The Thirteen Colonies

New Hampshire

Books in the Thirteen Colonies series include:

The Thirteen Colonies

New Hampshire

Craig E. Blohm

Lucent Books, Inc.
10911 Technology Place, San Diego, California 92127

For Eric and Jason

Library of Congress Cataloging-in-Publication Data

Blohm, Craig E., 1948–
  New Hampshire / by Craig E. Blohm.
    p. cm. — (The thirteen colonies)
  Includes bibliographical references and index.
  Summary: Discusses the founding of New Hampshire, daily life and
politics in the early years, its role in the American Revolution, and its
achievement of statehood.
  ISBN 1-56006-991-0 (alk. paper)
  1. New Hampshire—History—Colonial period, ca. 1600–1775—
Juvenile literature. 2. New Hampshire—History—1775–1865—
Juvenile literature. [1. New Hampshire—History—Colonial period,
ca. 1600–1775. 2. New Hampshire—History—1775–1865.] I. Title. II.
Series Thirteen colonies (Lucent Books).
  F37 .B58 2002
  974.2'02—dc21
                                                              2001003623

Copyright 2002 by Lucent Books, Inc.
10911 Technology Place, San Diego, California 92127

Printed in the U.S.A.

Contents

Foreword

The story of the thirteen English colonies that became the United States of America is one of startling diversity, conflict, and cultural evolution. Today, it is easy to assume that the colonists were of one mind when fighting for independence from England and afterwards when the national government was created. However, the American colonies had to overcome a vast reservoir of distrust rooted in the broad geographical, economic, and social differences that separated them. Even the size of the colonies contributed to the conflict; the smaller states feared domination by the larger ones.

These sectional differences stemmed from the colonies' earliest days. The northern colonies were more populous and their economies were more diverse, being based on both agriculture and manufacturing. The southern colonies, however, were dependent on agriculture—in most cases, the export of only one or two staple crops. These economic differences led to disagreements over things such as the trade embargo the Continental Congress imposed against England during the war. The southern colonies wanted their staple crops to be exempt from the embargo because their economies would have collapsed if they could not trade with England, which in some cases was the sole importer. A compromise was eventually made and the southern colonies were allowed to keep trading some exports.

In addition to clashing over economic issues, often the colonies did not see eye to eye on basic political philosophy. For example, Connecticut leaders held that education was the route to greater political liberty, believing that knowledgeable citizens would not allow themselves to be stripped of basic freedoms and rights. South Carolinians, on the other hand, thought that the protection of personal property and economic independence was the basic foundation of freedom. In light of such profound differences it is amazing that the colonies were able to unite in the fight for independence and then later under a strong national government.

Why, then, did the colonies unite? When the Revolutionary War began the colonies set aside their differences and banded together because they shared a common goal—political freedom from what they considered a tyrannical monarchy—that could be more easily attained if they cooperated with each other. However, after the war ended, the states abandoned unity and once again pursued sectional interests, functioning as little nations in a weak confederacy. The congress of this confederacy, which was bound by the Articles of Confederation, had virtually no authority over the individual states. Much bickering ensued—the individual states refused to pay their war debts to the national government, the nation was sinking further into an economic depression, and there was nothing the national government could do. Political leaders realized that the nation was in jeopardy of falling apart. They were also aware that European nations such as England, France, and Spain were all watching the new country, ready to conquer it at the first opportunity. Thus the states came together at the Constitutional Convention in order to create a system of government that would be strong enough to protect them from invasion and yet non-threatening to state interests and individual liberties.

The Thirteen Colonies series affords the reader a thorough understanding of how the development of the individual colonies helped create the United States. The series examines the early history of each colony's geographical region, the founding and first years of each colony, daily life in the colonies, and each colony's role in the American Revolution. Emphasis is given to the political, economic, and social uniqueness of each colony. Both primary and secondary quotes enliven the text, and sidebars highlight personalities, legends, and personal stories. Each volume ends with a chapter on how the colony dealt with changes after the war and its role in developing the U.S. Constitution and the new nation. Together, the books in this series convey a remarkable story—how thirteen fiercely independent colonies came together in an unprecedented political experiment that not only succeeded, but endures to this day.

Introduction

"Live Free or Die"

In 1809, eighty-one-year-old General John Stark was invited to a reunion to celebrate the thirty-second anniversary of the Battle of Bennington, in which he had led his troops to victory and paved the way for America's ultimate triumph in the Revolutionary War. Although Stark could not attend the reunion because of poor health, he wrote a letter of greeting to those in attendance. He ended the letter with a toast to be said at the banquet: "Live free or die; Death is not the worst of evils."[1]

It was a sentiment befitting the tough New Hampshire men who had bravely battled the British and their Hessian mercenaries so long before. The next year, in an invitation to another banquet, one of Stark's comrades wrote to him: "The toast, sir, which you sent us in 1809 will continue to vibrate with unceasing pleasure in our ears."[2] Indeed, Stark's words continued to vibrate into modern times. In 1945, the New Hampshire legislature made the first part of Stark's toast, "Live Free or Die," the state's official motto. Today these stirring words live on as a part of New Hampshire's official state emblem, appearing below an image of the famous rock formation the "Old Man of the Mountain." But they also live on in the hearts of New Hampshireites who cherish the colonial heritage of their state.

The people of New Hampshire are Yankees through and through, rugged New Englanders who are hardworking, resourceful, and fiercely proud of their independence. These character traits go all the way back to colonial times and to people such as John Mason, who first settled New Hampshire and named it after his home county in England; John Stark, Revolutionary War general; Josiah Bartlett, signer of the Declaration of Independence; and John Langdon, the first U.S. senator from New Hampshire. But for every famous figure in New Hampshire history, there were thousands of

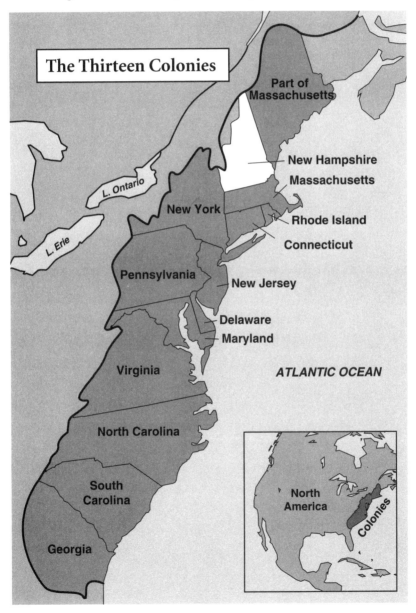

ordinary people whose labor made the state what it is today: fishermen and farmers, teachers and factory workers, seamstresses and shipbuilders, and a myriad of others for whom "Live Free or Die" was a way of life.

Although New Hampshire remained almost last in population during the colonial period (even today the state ranks forty-fourth in the nation), it was the first to vote for independence and was the state whose ratification made the U.S. Constitution official. Though its seacoast stretches only eighteen miles, colonial New Hampshire boasted a thriving seaport that traded around the world and whose shipyards built countless vessels for commerce and war. And while no revolutionary battle was fought in the state, the first armed attack against the British occurred in New Hampshire, months before the fighting at Lexington and Concord, Massachusetts, marked the start of the revolution.

America is the freest nation on earth, yet we often take our precious freedom for granted. It is easy to forget that we owe our liberty to brave people like the colonists of New Hampshire, who faced incredible hardships in the early years of our country's existence. "Live Free or Die" is a fitting tribute to those who died building a nation so that we, today, might live free.

Chapter One

Early New Hampshire

The first inhabitants of the vast region that would one day be known as New England did not arrive in lofty sailing ships. They did not come to create a new nation, nor to search for great wealth; neither were they fleeing religious intolerance. They came seeking new hunting grounds as the glaciers retreated. They called themselves the original people, and their legends told of a great mythical giant who gave them the land in all its abundance.

The people lived peaceful lives, preferring to trade with their neighbors rather than fight them. They inhabited the land for thousands of years before others arrived from across the ocean, this time with ships and guns and sickness. The original people of New Hampshire would be displaced by the white people who came from Europe with hopes and dreams the Native Americans could not understand: hopes of wealth and dreams of conquest.

People of the Dawnland

The Native Americans who first migrated to the eastern part of North America belonged to a language group known as Algonquian. Numerous Algonquian tribes lived along the coast from as far south as present-day North Carolina to the northern reaches of New Brunswick in Canada. The tribes that inhabited northern New

The original people of New Hampshire came seeking new hunting grounds they believed were granted by a great mythical giant.

England were known as Wabanaki, or people of the Dawnland, for they were the first to welcome each new day as the sun rose above the eastern shore.

Included within the Wabanaki were the Abenaki tribes, divided into two groups: the eastern Abenaki in Maine, and the western Abenaki in Vermont and New Hampshire. Tribes within the Abenaki included, among others, the Pennacook, Ossipee, Piscataqua, Winnepesaukee, and Nashua. By the year 1600, some ten thousand western Abenaki lived in New Hampshire and Vermont.

The Abenaki depended mainly on hunting and fishing for their basic sustenance. Captain John Josselyn, an English naturalist who observed the Native Americans of New England, wrote an account of an Abenaki moose hunt:

> When the snow will bear them, the young and lusty Indians (leaving their [children] and old people at home) go forth to hunt moose, deer, bear and beaver, thirty or forty miles up into the country; when they light upon a moose they run him down, which is sometimes in half a day . . . at last

they go up to him on each side and transpierce him with their lances . . . the poor creature groans, and walks on heavily, for a space, then sinks and falls down like a ruined building, making the earth to quake.[3]

In the spring and summer, coastal areas provided shellfish and lobsters, while rivers and streams were abundant with cod, bass, and salmon. New Hampshire's cool climate and short growing

America's Stonehenge

About forty miles north of Boston in North Salem, New Hampshire, stands a complex of huge stone structures dating back some four thousand years. Discovered by European settlers in the seventeenth century, the thirty-acre site is called America's Stonehenge, a reference to its similarity, in purpose if not design, to its famous counterpart in England.

The megaliths, or huge stones, of America's Stonehenge are arranged to form a series of dwellings, underground chambers, walls, and tunnels that have been given such names as the Oracle Chamber, the Watch House, and the Upton Chamber. The stones weigh up to eleven tons, which raises the question of how primitive people could build such structures. We may never know the answer to that question, or to the mystery of why America's Stonehenge was built. Most archaeologists who have studied it believe that it is an ancient calendar and astronomical observatory. Several standing stones, or monoliths, are positioned to align with the sun at the summer and winter solstices; others form alignments with the moon or various stars.

But there was perhaps a more sinister aspect to the site as well. One five-ton slab rests like a table on four stone legs, with shallow grooves cut around the edges of the table's surface. This structure is known as the Sacrificial Table, and the grooves may have carried human blood to waiting receptacles.

Who built America's Stonehenge? No one knows for sure. But whoever they were, and whatever their purposes may have been, they remain an ancient, enigmatic part of the history of New Hampshire.

season limited the crops the Abenaki could cultivate to corn, squash, and beans. A wide variety of nuts and berries gathered by the tribe's women and children rounded out the Abenaki diet.

Most Abenaki families lived in wigwams, dome-shaped structures made of bent saplings covered with birch bark or mats of woven rushes. These dwellings were easily dismantled for seasonal travel. The Abenaki also built larger, more permanent buildings called longhouses. These were described by a French missionary visiting an Abenaki village in the 1600s as "long and covered with the bark of trees of all kinds. The top is domed, with a hole over each fire to let out the smoke."[4] A longhouse could be one hundred feet in length and accommodate up to eight families. For protection from such neighboring hostile tribes as the Mohawk, Abenaki villages were surrounded by a stockade of sturdy pine logs towering some twelve feet above the ground.

The Abenaki built longhouse villages surrounded by a stockade of towering pine logs.

Abenaki religious beliefs included a variety of spirits, or manitous, from sun, moon, and wind gods to malevolent underwater spirits waiting to ensnare an unsuspecting fisherman. Many Abenaki wore amulets or charms made of stone, animal teeth, or shells to ward off evil spirits. These amulets were also believed to imbue the warriors' weapons with magical power to make them more effective in battle.

Medicine men called shamans were said to be able to communicate with the Abenaki spirits. Dressed in the costume of a bird or beast, the shaman used his powers to drive out evil spirits thought to inhabit a person's body and cause illness. But for all their powers, no shaman could have foreseen how Abenaki life would change with the coming of Europeans to the shores of the Dawnland.

"Walking Islands"

Seeing the first European sailing ships approach the rugged New England coast must have filled the native population with both wonder and fear. For a people who had little notion of a greater world outside of their own, it was an experience they could comprehend only in terms of their own knowledge. One Algonquian tribe called the first ships "walking islands." According to a contemporary account by William Wood, they took "the mast to be a tree, the saile white clouds, and the discharging of ordnance [ammunition] for lightning and thunder."[5]

One of the first European arrivals was Italian explorer Giovanni Caboto, better known by the English name John Cabot, who crossed the Atlantic in 1497 under the sponsorship of King Henry VII. After landing in Newfoundland, Cabot sailed his vessel down the coast, past New Hampshire as far south as Virginia, eventually returning to England with tales of the forests and rivers of his "new found land." After Cabot, many sixteenth-century fishermen braved the perils of the North Atlantic to fish off the coast of Newfoundland. These fishermen may also have visited the coastal waters of New Hampshire, although there is no evidence that they actually did.

A business venture to search for the aromatic sassafras tree brought the first recorded visit of a European explorer to New

John Cabot landed in America in what the Algonquian called "walking islands."

Hampshire. In 1603, a group of merchants in Bristol, England, hired Captain Martin Pring to journey to the new world and bring back sassafras roots, which were thought to have medicinal properties. Commanding two ships, the *Speedwell* and the *Discoverer,* Pring sailed down the coast of Maine to New Hampshire. Upon reaching the mouth of the Piscataqua River he turned his ships westward and sailed ten or twelve miles up the river searching for the valuable sassafras. "In all these places," Pring later wrote, "we found no people, but signs of fires where they had been. . . . [W]e beheld very goodly groves and woods replenished with tall oaks, beeches, pine trees, fir trees, hazels, witch-hazels and maples. We saw here also sundry sorts of beasts, as stags, deer, bears, wolves, foxes, lucernes [lynx], and dogs. But meeting with no sassafras, we left these places."[6] Pring continued south along the coast of Massachusetts and eventually found enough sassafras to fill the holds of his ships. He returned home with a valuable cargo and the first recorded account of a European visit to New Hampshire.

Two years after Martin Pring's voyage, French explorer Samuel de Champlain sailed along the New Hampshire coastline. "Two leagues to the east," Champlain wrote, "we saw three or four rather high islands, and on the west a large bay."[7] The islands Champlain described were the Isles of Shoals, situated some ten miles off New

Hampshire's coast. Later, while exploring the area of the Merrimack River, Champlain encountered groups of Native Americans, to whom he gave small presents. He found nut trees and grapevines, and learned that the native inhabitants "cultivated the land and sowed seeds like the others, who we had before seen."[8]

Champlain told of discovering a large body of water known as the "Lake of the Iroquois," which was probably New Hampshire's large Lake Winnepesaukee. He may also have seen the distant peaks of the White Mountains. But Samuel de Champlain was an explorer, not a colonizer. One man who became impassioned about colonizing the New World was Captain John Smith.

Fish and Furs

John Smith, an adventurer and soldier of fortune, was president of the first permanent English settlement in North America, the Jamestown colony, founded in Virginia in 1607. After returning to England to recover from a serious injury, he set sail in 1614 on another voyage to America. With two ships, the *Frances* and the *Queen Anne*, Captain Smith explored the northern coast of North America, including what would eventually be New Hampshire. According to Jeremy Belknap, New Hampshire's first historian,

Determined to create a permanent settlement, John Smith helped build the Jamestown colony.

Smith "ranged the shore from Penobscot to Cape Cod, and in this route discovered the river Piscataqua; which he found to be a safe harbor with a rocky shore."[9] The area around the Piscataqua would become home for the first settlements in New Hampshire.

Captain Smith's visit to North America was to be a commercial venture. "Our plot," he wrote, "was there to take whales and make trials of a mine of gold and copper. If those failed, fish and furs was then our refuge."[10] His attempt at whaling was a costly failure, and gold and other metals were nowhere to be found. Smith and several others went exploring, ranging in small boats up and down the coast. Like Samuel de Champlain before him, Smith also encountered the Isles of Shoals off the New Hampshire coast. Unlike Champlain, however, Smith decided to personalize his discovery by naming the islands "Smith's Isles" after himself. In the waters around these rocky islands he discovered what would become one of the staples of New Hampshire's colonial economy: fish. According to his account Smith's fishermen were able to catch sixty thousand fish in just one month.

When Smith returned to England absorbed with the idea of colonizing the New World, he told his friends he was eager "to plant there a Colony, and make further search, and discovery in those parts there yet unknown."[11] Encouraged at least in part by John Smith's enthusiastic tales, sailing ships would soon be bringing colonists to New Hampshire. There the Europeans would clash with the Abenaki tribes already living on the land.

Europeans Ascendant

The Abenaki of New Hampshire lived in harmony with the land they inhabited. They looked upon it as a gift given to them by the spirits to live on and to use. To the European mind of the early seventeenth century, however, the land was a limitless source of natural resources there for the taking. It could be cultivated to produce commodities for commerce, and the land itself could be bought and sold as well. The Europeans did not understand the roaming nature of Abenaki existence, in which they moved from planting fields to coastal fishing areas to woodland hunting grounds as the seasons changed. European ideas of land ownership included setting boundaries, building fences, and levying taxes.

The colonists decided that the Native Americans had not "subdued" or tamed the land (according to European standards) and therefore had no right to possess it. In addition, the colonists did not recognize the legitimacy of native governing bodies and thus held that the Native Americans had no legal claim to the land on which they lived. So, the Europeans felt they had the right to take what they wanted. As more and more explorers began coming to America, they brought with them their own views of land ownership and property rights. They also brought something even more deadly.

When Europeans crossed the Atlantic they unwittingly carried to the New World influenza, smallpox, measles, scarlet fever, and other diseases that were common in Europe. Through generations of exposure to these afflictions in their homelands, the Europeans had for the most part become immune to them. But for Native Americans, who had not developed such immunity, the result was a series of epidemics that raged through the population and wiped out entire villages.

Unknowingly, the first European settlers carried disease, which would result in epidemics that would wipe out entire villages of Native Americans.

A Pennacook Powwow

His name was Papisseconewa, which means "son of the bear," but he was known to the English colonists as Passaconaway. Born sometime around the middle of the sixteenth century, Passaconaway became the *sachem,* or chief, of the Pennacook tribe that lived in the area of what is today Manchester, New Hampshire. Besides being the *sachem,* he was also a *powwow*—a medicine man. His powers were the stuff of which legends are made, as can be seen in this contemporary report reproduced in *New Hampshire: A Guide to the Granite State* by the Federal Writers' Project. According to this account, Passaconaway could "make the water burn, the rocks move, the trees dance, metamorphise himself into a flaming man . . . and make of a dead snake's skin a living snake, both to be seen, felt, and heard. This I write but upon the report of the Indians who confidently affirm stranger things."

For all his reputed powers, however, Passaconaway could not prevent the English from ultimately betraying him. In 1642, colonists fearing an attack by the Pennacooks kidnapped Passaconaway's son Wonalancet. The young man was later released, in return for which Passaconaway surrendered the tribe's weapons. Still, the great *sachem* advocated peace with the colonists. A few years before his death, Passaconaway gathered his people together and delivered a farewell speech. As recounted in *New Hampshire: A Guide to the Granite State*, his speech ended with the words "Peace, peace with the white man—is the command of the Great Spirit—and the wish—the last wish—of Passaconaway."

A devastating epidemic struck the Abenaki tribes of New Hampshire between 1616 and 1619. The disease could have been smallpox, measles, or perhaps scarlet fever. Since the Abenaki had no written language, no records exist of this period of their history, but some historians estimate that more than 75 percent of the tribes died as the disease swept through the region. Many Native Americans who survived fled westward in an effort to escape the scourge, leaving behind deserted villages, untended crops, and the unburied bodies of their relatives. These epidemics further paved the way for Europeans to take over Native American lands.

Native Americans in a Strange Land

Although Captain John Smith never again set foot in New England after his voyage in 1614, his enthusiastic words helped to ignite a spark of interest in colonizing the unexplored and seemingly limitless reaches of America. Among those he ultimately influenced was Sir Ferdinando Gorges, a man who would play a role in colonizing New Hampshire.

Ferdinando Gorges was the son of a wealthy English landowner and a soldier by profession. He was the military commander of Plymouth Fort, a defensive installation on the southwestern coast of England. Plymouth was a bustling seaport and Gorges encountered many explorers returning from America with tales of the riches to be found there. One of those explorers was George Weymouth who in 1605 returned from America with a cargo hold filled with furs and timber. He also brought back "five savages, two canoas [canoes] with all their bows and arrows."[12] Three of the Native Americans went to live with Gorges. For three years they stayed in Gorges's house, where they learned to speak English. Soon they were describing the wonders of their homeland to their fascinated host. Since it was a time of peace in England, military men like Gorges had fewer responsibilities to occupy their minds. So he began to consider the possibility of setting up colonies in the New World. As he later wrote, the three Native Americans who came to him in 1605 "must be acknowledged the means under God of putting on foot and giving life to all our plantations."[13]

Those plantations, or colonies, destroyed the way of life lived for centuries by the Abenaki tribes of New Hampshire. The "People of the Dawnland" were forced to make way for the European who came to the New World as explorer, colonist, and conqueror.

Chapter Two

Founding the Colony

By the early seventeenth century European interest in colonizing the New World seemed to reach a fever pitch. Spain and Portugal had already established vast empires stretching from Florida to the coasts of South America. France claimed land in North America that had been explored by Jacques Cartier in 1534 and 1535. Not to be outdone by their European rivals, English adventurers were poised to descend upon the New World.

The Council for New England

His interest in colonization stimulated by his three Native American guests, Sir Ferdinando Gorges became a part of the Virginia Company, which established the successful Jamestown colony in 1607. Between 1606 and 1608 the company made several attempts to send expeditions to New England. None of these ventures succeeded, however, for each time the explorers found the harsh climate a formidable obstacle to permanent settlement. Discouraged by these failures, Gorges's enthusiasm for planting a permanent colony in the New World waned.

That enthusiasm was revived when Captain John Smith returned from his 1614 voyage. In order to promote colonization, in 1615

Smith wrote a small book entitled *A Description of New-England*. The book was really a propaganda brochure, and in it Smith painted a glowing picture of the New World. In this passage, he writes about fishing, perhaps inspired by the abundant schools of fish he found around the Isles of Shoals:

If a man work but three days in seven, he may get more than he can spend, unless he will be excessive. Now that carpenter, mason, gardiner, tailor, smith, sailor, forgers, or what other, may they not make this a pretty recreation though they fish but an hour in a day to take more than they eat in a week? Or if they will not eat it because there is so much better choice, yet sell it or change it with the fishermen or merchants for anything they want. And what sport doth yield a more pleasing content, and less hurt or charge than angling with a hook, and crossing the sweet air

John Smith stands on the shores of the New World, about which he wrote the book *A Description of New-England*.

from isle to isle over the silent streams of a calm sea,
wherein the most curious may find pleasure, profit and
content?[14]

Gorges once more began thinking about colonization. But to put
those thoughts into action he needed permission from the Crown.
At that time, English adventurers had to seek royal authorization
to establish colonies in the New World. The king gave his consent
by issuing "charters," documents that granted land in America to
individuals or corporations. In November 1620, a group of forty
businessmen including Gorges was granted a charter to create an
organization named the Council for New England. The council was
established "for the planting, ruling, ordering, and governing of
New England, in America."[15] Sir Ferdinando Gorges was appointed
president of the council.

The Council for New England was authorized to issue grants for
planting colonies in North America between the fortieth and forty-
eighth parallel—a huge area essentially covering New York to
Maine. As Jeremy Belknap wrote, this authorization was "the
foundation of all the [land] grants that were made of the country
of New-England."[16] It was also the source of confusion that lasted
for more than a hundred years.

The attempt to divide up an unexplored land an ocean away
from England caused problems in defining boundaries for the
land grants. No accurate surveys of the New World existed. The
men of the Council for New England had never been to America,
and what they knew of the land came mainly from reports of
fishermen and traders who had been there. Thus the boundaries
were at best, approximations that often overlapped each other and
extended ill-defined borders into the wilderness. Even with an
official grant a landowner could never really be sure of the true
extent and boundaries of his property. Disputes were inevitable.
As Belknap commented in 1784, "the grants which they made were
so inaccurately described, and interfered so much with each other,
as to occasion difficulties and controversies, some of which are not
yet ended."[17]

Founding Dover

Some historians feel that David Thomson should share the honor of creating the first settlement in New Hampshire with two brothers named Hilton. Edward and William Hilton began founding their own colony about the time that Pannaway Plantation was being established. The Hilton brothers were London fishmongers, or sellers of fish, and like Pannaway their colony was to be based primarily on the fish trade. William Hilton had been living at the Plymouth Colony while his brother Edward resided at Pannaway. In the fall of 1623, the Hiltons moved seven miles up the Piscataqua River to a place called Winnichahannat by the Native Americans. The area would be known as Hilton's Point, and the colony they established there would eventually become the town of Dover.

The Dover colony prospered through fishing and the fur trade with Native Americans. But Edward and William Hilton actually had no legal grant for the land when they started the colony. In 1631, the Council for New England finally issued a formal patent to Edward Hilton. As reported by Jeremy Belknap in his *History of New-Hampshire,* the grant gave him "all that part of the river Piscataqua called or known by the name of Hilton's Point." This grant acknowledged that Hilton and his associates had established the Dover colony with their own money and intended to see to its continued prosperity.

Unaware of, or untroubled by, the future difficulties they were creating, the Council for New England granted more than a dozen patents for colonization to its members between March 1622 and June 1623. One of the largest grants went to a young merchant named David Thomson.

Pannaway Plantation

David Thomson (sometimes spelled Thompson) was an English gentleman, an experienced mariner who had also worked as an apothecary, or pharmacist. In 1623, the Council for New England granted to Thomson one island and six thousand acres of land in New England. The location Thomson chose for his colony was

Odiorne's Point, a tip of land near a small harbor just south of the Piscataqua River. He called the plantation "Pannaway," a Native American name meaning "Little Harbor." Thomson and his colonists built a fortified house surrounded by a palisade and containing guns and ammunition for protection from possible Native American raids. They also constructed a blacksmith shop and living quarters for the colony's workers. On a nearby hill they built several "stages," or wooden platforms, on which to dry the fish that would be the basis of Pannaway's livelihood.

With abundant fish to catch and Native Americans to trade furs and hides with, the Pannaway Plantation was the earliest permanent European settlement in New Hampshire. When Thomson's wife, Amias, joined her husband she became New Hampshire's first white female resident. But the Pannaway Plantation did not last long. For unknown reasons David Thomson and his family left after a few years to take up residence on an island in Boston Harbor. There he contracted a serious

Colonists from the Pannaway Plantation follow an Algonquian guide.

illness and died. Without Thomson's leadership, the Pannaway Plantation eventually went bankrupt.

Although David Thomson may have been first to colonize New Hampshire, another adventurer, John Mason, named it and made a more permanent contribution to its development.

New Hampshire

Captain John Mason was a merchant and naval officer, and had spent the years from 1615 to 1621 in Newfoundland as the governor of the English plantation there. He was an enthusiastic proponent of colonization and in 1621 joined the Council for New England. He applied for a grant in America and was given a tract of land between the Salem and Merrimack Rivers, which he named "Mariana." Financially unable to colonize this tract, Mason then decided to partner with Sir Ferdinando Gorges. In 1622, they received a joint grant of "all the lands between the rivers Merrimack and Sagadehock [Kennebec], extending back to the great lakes and river of Canada."[18] This large territory extended some sixty miles into the unexplored interior of America.

In 1629, Gorges and Mason agreed to divide their large grant of land between them. The territory that Gorges retained would eventually become part of Maine. Mason's portion encompassed the land situated between the Piscataqua and Merrimack Rivers, which included approximately eighteen miles of Atlantic seacoast. Although already owner of the land as his part of the joint grant, Mason apparently wanted to reconfirm his ownership. On November 7, 1629, a new grant for the region was issued to Mason by the Council for New England for the purpose of "making a plantation and establishing of a colony or colonies in the country called or known by the name of New England in America."[19] Mason named his territory New Hampshire after Hampshire County in England, where he made his home.

John Mason soon made plans to send a group of colonists to New Hampshire under the auspices of an organization named the Laconia Company. The purpose of the company, established by Mason and

Early New Hampshire colonists relied on the lumbering industry as an important source of revenue.

Ferdinando Gorges along with other English investors, was to colonize and manage their territory in America. The investors hoped to reap a handsome profit by selling furs and fish from America to waiting markets in Europe. Having a permanent working colony in New Hampshire would eliminate time spent sailing to and from England, time that could be more profitably used fishing and trapping. As with most adventurers, Mason would be an absentee landlord and administer the colony from his home in England.

The eighty-ton vessel *Warwick,* carrying Mason's first group of colonists, arrived in America in the spring of 1630. Under the steady hand of Captain Walter Neale, the *Warwick* sailed slowly up the Piscataqua and finally dropped anchor about two miles from the mouth of the river. The colonists were enchanted by the abundance of wild strawberries they saw along the riverbank and decided that this was where they would make their plantation. They named their new home Strawbery Banke. The colonists constructed several buildings at Strawbery Banke, including a stone "great house" to serve as a residence and trading center. The Strawbery Banke colonists fished, hunted, and planted crops. Lumbering and trading with the Native Americans in the area were also important sources of revenue; Jeremy Belknap describes a colonist who "had the care of a sawmill, and lived in a palisaded house in Newichwannock, where he carried on trade with the Indians."[20] The colony began to prosper, and within ten years there were some 170 people living at Strawbery Banke.

Sir Ferdinando Gorges and Captain John Mason soon learned that colonizing a new world was an expensive undertaking, and profitably harvesting the natural treasures of New England would take longer than they had anticipated. Their business partners expected a quick return on their investment, however, and soon became dissatisfied with the slow profits, despite the success of Strawbery Banke. In late 1633 or early 1634, the Laconia Company was dissolved. Over the years Captain John Mason had spent £22,000 supplying his colonists with food, tools, fishing nets, guns and ammunition, and other necessities from England. Ultimately he had little to show for his investment. In 1635, Mason wrote to his New Hampshire colonists, "I have disbursed a great deal of money in the plantation, and never received one penny; but hope . . . that I should, in some reasonable time, be reimbursed again."[21] Mason's hopes would not be realized, however, for he died in December 1635.

John Mason's legacy included not only the colony named New Hampshire, but confusion caused by the various overlapping and inaccurate patents granted through the years. After Mason's death, many people simply claimed ownership of the New Hampshire lands they were living on. No one really knew who owned what. During all this confusion New Hampshire's neighbor to the south, Massachusetts Bay, was becoming New England's most powerful colony. Its success would have a profound impact on New Hampshire.

Puritans in New England

Men like Sir Ferdinando Gorges and Captain John Mason sought to colonize New England for commercial reasons. But not everyone looked at the New World as a place to do business; for a group known as the Puritans, America meant a chance for religious freedom. Distressed by the moral corruption and Roman Catholic influences they saw in the Church of England, the Puritans felt led to "purify" the church and society as well. The English government opposed these reforms and soon began persecuting the Puritans.

To escape this persecution, in 1629 they formed the Massachusetts Bay Company and obtained a charter from King Charles I for land in New England. A fleet of eleven ships carrying seven hundred Puritan men, women, and children sailed from England in 1630, led by John Winthrop aboard the flagship *Arbella*. They landed in New England and founded the Massachusetts Bay Colony as a place where they could enjoy religious freedom. Throughout the 1630s, English colonists arrived there in great numbers, making Massachusetts Bay the most populous colony in New England. Gradually some residents of Massachusetts began moving north to New Hampshire. Some came looking for new opportunities to make their fortunes while others, like John Wheelwright, were forced from Massachusetts after discovering that religious freedom there did not mean freedom for everyone.

Reverend John Wheelwright was a Puritan minister in Boston who was banished from Massachusetts in 1638 for speaking out against church doctrine. Along with a group of followers, Wheelwright headed north to establish his own settlement on land he had purchased from the Native Americans. The community he founded became the town of Exeter, New Hampshire. In 1639, another town named Hampton was established when Massachusetts laid claim to land in southern New Hampshire and granted a tract to Stephen Batchelor, another Puritan minister, and his congregation. "They began the settlement," wrote Jeremy Belknap, "by laying out a township in one hundred and forty-seven shares; and having formed a church chose Stephen Batchelor for their minister. . . . The number of the first inhabitants was fifty-six."[22]

By 1640, four towns had been established in New Hampshire: Strawbery Banke, Dover, Exeter, and Hampton. These four small communities, with a combined population of about one thousand, would remain the only towns in New Hampshire until 1675. Since Hampton was officially part of Massachusetts, it was the only one of the four towns to have a larger entity looking out for it. The

John Winthrop stands aboard the flagship *Arbella* off the shore of Massachusetts before landing in 1630.

Lacking the protection of Massachusetts, a Puritan family defends itself against a Native American raid.

other three towns had to fend for themselves against possible Native American raids and the lack of dependable support from England.

With the continuing confusion over land ownership, and without the guiding hand of John Mason, the New Hampshire towns realized that they needed some form of governing body. So they looked toward the strong and prosperous Massachusetts Bay Colony. In October 1641, the towns around the Piscataqua River petitioned the Crown to become part of Massachusetts. Dover was the first town officially annexed, followed by Exeter in 1643. Strawbery Banke (which would change its name to Portsmouth in 1653) was the last of the three towns to be annexed. Thus, by the middle of the seventeenth century, New Hampshire was under the authority of the Massachusetts legislature, called the General Court.

New Hampshire and Massachusetts

New Hampshire now had some political stability, adopting Massachusetts's form of township government. Town meetings were held and local citizens voted on such matters as laws, religion, and education. Two deputies represented each New Hampshire town in the Massachusetts General Court. The economy of the region grew as more Massachusetts people migrated north; agricultural activity

Rogers' Rangers

The French and Indian War was the final conflict in a series of wars that lasted for seventy-five years, from 1689 to 1754. England and France fought these wars to determine which country would rule North America. New Hampshire played a role in this conflict through an elite force known as Rogers' Rangers.

Robert Rogers was born in Massachusetts but grew up in New Hampshire, where frequent Native American raids taught him the value of such skills as tracking, camouflage, and fighting in natural surroundings. In 1755, possibly to avoid imprisonment for his part in a counterfeiting scheme, Rogers joined a New Hampshire regiment fighting for the Crown. He soon formed his own volunteer "ranging company" and taught them his style of frontier fighting. Dressed in buckskin and moccasins, Rogers' Rangers silently marched single file through the countryside, swiftly striking their Native American enemy and then melting back into the forest.

Rogers' Rangers conducted daring and successful raids throughout the war and led important scouting missions for the British army. In 1758, Rogers suffered his worst defeat at Lake George, New York, when the Rangers were ambushed by a superior force of Native Americans and Canadian troops. Rogers lost 125 troops and barely escaped with his own life. The Rangers regrouped and the next year attacked an Abenaki village at St. Francis in Canada in reprisal for Native Americans' raids on colonial villages. The Rangers burned the village to the ground.

By the end of the French and Indian War, Robert Rogers had become the most famous soldier in colonial America and a fitting example of the toughness of New Hampshire's people.

increased, and new mills for grinding grain and sawing lumber were built. Massachusetts also encouraged exploration of the western regions of New Hampshire.

Still, the people of New Hampshire retained their independent temperament, especially in regard to religion. The strict Puritanism of Massachusetts contrasted with a more tolerant attitude in New Hampshire. While church membership was necessary in order to vote in Massachusetts, no such requirement applied in New Hampshire. Quakers, persecuted and banned from Massachusetts, found refuge in New Hampshire. Although witchcraft trials raged in Massachusetts in the late 1600s, only one person, Goodwife Walford, was ever tried in New Hampshire. Not only was she acquitted of the charge of witchcraft, she was awarded damages from her accusers.

New Hampshire continued under the administration of Massachusetts for nearly forty years. But that would change in 1679

New Hampshire colonists exhibited a tolerant attitude toward religious freedom.

by a proclamation from England's King Charles II, and a petition by an heir of Captain John Mason.

A Royal Colony

Robert Tufton Mason was the captain's grandson and heir to the New Hampshire territory. In an effort to clear up the land grant confusion once and for all, in 1660 he petitioned the Crown to investigate his claim that he was the rightful owner of New Hampshire. After years of languishing in the English courts, the petition had come to nothing. Discouraged, Mason was ready to give up when, by chance, the king of England breathed new life into his efforts.

In 1672, King Charles II learned that Massachusetts wanted to purchase the land grants covering Maine and New Hampshire. The king thought that the Bay Colony was overstepping its authority, so he decided it was time to assert stronger royal control over Massachusetts. Upon hearing this, Mason renewed his efforts to declare his ownership of New Hampshire. More years of court battles ensued, but in July 1679, the matter was finally settled in Mason's favor. Jeremy Belknap reports that "the colony of Massachusetts was informed, by a letter from the secretary of state, of the king's intention to separate New-Hampshire from their government, and required to revoke all commissions which they had granted there, and which were hereby declared null and void."[23] Robert Mason obtained ownership of all unimproved property in John Mason's original New Hampshire grant, and could collect rent from all those who lived on his land. With Massachusetts chastened, the English government obtained stronger control over all of the colonies. On September 18, the seal of the Crown made it official: New Hampshire was now a royal colony. Although aged and somewhat infirm, John Cutt, a wealthy merchant and prominent citizen of New Hampshire, was appointed president.

In January 1680, President John Cutt and his deputies took their oaths of office and established the government of the new royal colony of New Hampshire. The new colony had at its beginning a population of about two thousand. Growth would occur gradually over the next century; New Hampshire's population numbered only about eighty thousand by the time of the American Revolution. Native American raids, continuing boundary disputes, and the difficulty of carving a home out of the wilderness were all factors in New Hampshire's slow expansion. But these same factors also assured that the people who settled and built their lives in this rugged colony were the truly hardy souls that would come to represent the spirit of New Hampshire.

Chapter Three

Life in Colonial New Hampshire

To the English businessmen who financed colonizing expeditions to North America in the seventeenth century, New Hampshire must have seemed like a paradise just waiting to be conquered by hardy and adventurous souls. In his *The History of New-Hampshire*, Jeremy Belknap recounts one explorer's imaginative description of New Hampshire with its "air pure and salubrious; the country pleasant, having some high hills; full of goodly forests, fair valleys and fertile plains; abounding in corn, vines, chestnuts, and many other sorts of fruits; the rivers well stored with fish, and environed with goodly meadows full of timber trees."[24] As idyllic as this report sounded, however, the reality of life in colonial New Hampshire proved to be quite a different story.

Harnessing the Forest

The Englishmen and women who colonized New Hampshire were no strangers to work. Being so far away from their homeland, they knew that they would have to be more self-sufficient than they had ever been before, merely to survive. In the beginning survival meant finding shelter from the elements, and for that the colonists turned to New Hampshire's most abundant natural resource: trees. A wide

To find shelter, New Hampshire's colonists harnessed the forests to make homes out of the wilderness.

variety of trees—pine, birch, maple, cedar, and many others—covered the New Hampshire landscape. As the colonists cleared the land to make room for planting crops, they sawed the felled trees into boards which were then used to build small frame houses.

Besides providing shelter, New Hampshire's abundant forests also became a major source of income for the colony. The fishermen along the coast needed boats to pursue their trade, and the forests of New Hampshire furnished the raw materials to build fishing schooners, whaleboats, and other types of working vessels. Swiftly flowing rivers supplied power for the sawmills necessary to convert logs into planks for making boats. As the demand for lumber increased, more and more mills were established until, by 1700, some ninety sawmills were supplying shipyards with their products. New Hampshire shipbuilders also constructed ships for the British merchant marine, as well as passenger vessels that sailed regular routes up and down the New England coast. Of the New Hampshire shipbuilding industry, Jeremy Belknap wrote "There are no workmen more capable of constructing good ships than the carpenters of New Hampshire. But the goodness of a ship ever did and will depend on the quality of the materials."[25] New Hampshire was fortunate to have one of the finest materials for the shipping industry: tall, straight pine trees that were of particular value to the British navy.

"The white pine of the forest," commented Belknap, "is the strongest and most durable timber which America affords for masts."[26] Soaring some 150 to 200 feet tall, New Hampshire's mast pines towered over surrounding trees. The pines chosen to be felled for masts were marked by British surveyors, who branded the trunks with three ax cuts known as the King's Broad Arrow. Anyone who illegally cut down Broad Arrow trees risked prosecution and a £100 fine. Sent to England in special ships, the mast pines were important to the British navy because they lasted four times longer than other mast woods used at that time on British warships. The

An abundance of trees made New Hampshire an important part of the shipbuilding industry.

A New Hampshire Dynasty

The name Wentworth figures prominently in New Hampshire history, for the colony was ruled by three members of that family for most of the period from 1717 until the eve of the Revolution. John Wentworth, born in 1671, was lieutenant governor of Massachusetts during the time that colony controlled New Hampshire. Wentworth lived in New Hampshire and served as administrator of the colony until his death in 1730.

Benning Wentworth became the first royal governor of New Hampshire when it was finally liberated from the control of Massachusetts in 1741. The son of John Wentworth, Benning was born in Portsmouth and attended Harvard College (later Harvard University) in Massachusetts. An ambitious governor, he lived an elegant life in New Hampshire, building a mansion in Portsmouth and entertaining frequently. Benning financed his lavish lifestyle by granting huge parcels of New Hampshire land to his friends and keeping five hundred acres of each grant for himself. Many New Hampshireites felt he was just too greedy, and Wentworth was forced to resign in 1767. He relinquished his office to his nephew, John.

Also a Harvard graduate, John Wentworth spent several years in England looking after the family business. When his uncle Benning resigned, John took over and soon became a popular governor of the colony. He advocated the development of New Hampshire's interior and helped establish Dartmouth College. But his popularity began to decline as the colonies' revolutionary spirit grew. In 1775, John Wentworth and his family were forced to flee Portsmouth, bringing an end to the Wentworth dynasty in New Hampshire.

mast trade was one of the colony's most important businesses, and made fortunes for many Portsmouth entrepreneurs. But not everyone in the colony lived a rich life. For the typical farmer, life was as tough as the rocky New Hampshire soil.

Working Men and Women

For most colonists in New Hampshire, farming became a way of life. But while the Merrimack and Connecticut River valleys provided fertile agricultural land, most of New Hampshire's soil was hard and rocky. Before this ground could be planted, large rocks left in the fields by receding glaciers thousands of years before had to be moved. Farmers piled the rocks on top of each other to make sturdy stone walls to separate their property from their neighbors' lands. These walls became a symbol of the New Hampshire farmer's devotion to hard work and determination to overcome even the most difficult obstacles that stood in his way.

Once the fields were cleared, cultivation of the land could begin. Working with the same kinds of hand tools—hoes, scythes, and pitchforks—their ancestors used, New Hampshire farmers prepared fields for planting corn, beans, and squash. These crops were planted Native American style in mounds, with the corn on top, then the beans, and the squash last, with a fish put in each mound as fertilizer. The potato became an important crop in the colonies when introduced by Scotch-Irish immigrants who founded Londonderry in 1719.

The men handled the farming chores, which was backbreaking work but had to be done regardless of the weather or the toughness

Before the land of New Hampshire could be planted, farmers had to remove large rocks left by receding glaciers.

New Hampshire farmers prepared fields for planting corn, beans, and squash, using the same kinds of tools their ancestors used.

of the soil. Women had their work to do as well, chores that were no less important than the men's. A colonial woman's day was filled with tending the garden, preparing meals, spinning wool for clothing, making soap and candles, and rearing the children. "The people in these times were a very plain people," wrote Reverend David Sutherland, a minister in Bath, New Hampshire, "dressing in homespun cloth. Every house had its loom and spinning-wheel, and almost every woman was a weaver."[27] But colonial housewives suffered from the tedium of their housebound jobs. While their husbands' tasks changed with the seasons and often involved hunting or fishing trips, the women's work truly was never done, nor did it change much from day to day or year to year.

Labor continued six days a week for the people of colonial New Hampshire. But on the seventh day, the Sabbath, work gave way to worship.

Religion in New Hampshire

Although the New Hampshire colony was established for commercial rather than religious reasons, religion nonetheless played an important role in the colony. Life in New Hampshire was centered around the town, and each town was centered around the church, or meetinghouse. Constructed by the townspeople and financed by taxes, the meetinghouse accommodated both religious services and town meetings, where the business of the colony could be discussed. Ministers had been in the colony from the earliest times, but the first meetinghouse was probably built in Hampton in 1639. As New Hampshire's population increased more meetinghouses were built, and by the middle of the eighteenth century there were more than sixty in the colony. Larger towns such as Portsmouth often had more than one meetinghouse. On Sunday mornings the people gathered at the meetinghouse for worship. "People who owned horses rode them," wrote Reverend Sutherland, "and those who had them not went on foot. Husbands carried their wives behind them on pillions [saddles]. More than one half of the church-going people went on foot. Sleighs or sleds were used in winter. I have seen ox-sleds at the meeting-house. For years we had no stoves in the meeting-house of Bath; and yet in the coldest weather, the house was always full."[28]

The services usually lasted all day with the minister preaching more than one sermon. The congregation sang hymns from the Bay Psalm Book and took up collections for the needy. During respites from organized worship, the colonists shared town news, observations on the weather and, of course, a bit of gossip. Often churchgoers meted out punishment to individuals found guilty of straying from the town's social norms—reprimands that could range from a simple rebuke to banishment from the fellowship.

Most New Hampshireites were members of the Congregational Church, the church of the Massachusetts Bay pilgrims. But unlike the Massachusetts Bay colony, early New Hampshire was fairly tolerant of other religions. Many people, such as John Wheelwright, who disagreed with the authoritarian Puritans in Massachusetts found New Hampshire a more broad-minded place in which to live. Eventually New Hampshire became home to Presbyterians, Episcopalians, Baptists, and Quakers. The latter group migrated to New Hampshire seeking refuge from the harsh penalties that

Churchgoers walk through an icy forest on their way to the meetinghouse.

Massachusetts imposed on them because of their beliefs. Despite some periods of persecution, the Quaker church grew in New Hampshire and eventually comprised one-third of the churches in the town of Dover.

When not being used for religious services, the meetinghouse played another important role in the life of New Hampshire. For it was here that the townspeople assembled to discuss the important matters of governing their colony.

Governing New Hampshire

After New Hampshire became a royal colony under the rule of King Charles II of England in 1679, the king appointed a governor to oversee the affairs of the colony. The governor ruled with the assistance of a council, also chosen by the Crown. As in the other colonies, New Hampshire had an elected assembly, which represented the interests of the people. At local town meetings those eligible to vote (usually male landowners) made decisions on laws, taxes, education, and other matters directly concerning the community. While the citizens handled local affairs, the royal governor concerned himself with matters that affected the whole colony. Many of New Hampshire's governors, however, were so tyrannical that in 1698 New Hampshire once more aligned itself with Massachusetts and was ruled by that colony's governor until 1741. Of all New Hampshire's royal governors, none had more influence than Benning Wentworth and his nephew John Wentworth, who successively governed the colony for thirty-four years.

Laws in colonial New Hampshire addressed a myriad of transgressions, and punishment could be harsh for those who ran afoul of them. Murder, of course, was punishable by death, as were witchcraft, treason, manstealing (kidnapping), and arson. Slander, or verbal assault, was made a crime in a society where civility and respect were necessary for keeping society together. Drunkenness was perhaps the most prevalent crime throughout New England. Public intoxication was punished by locking the accused in the stocks, a wooden frame that shackled a person's hands or feet and served to hold an offender up to public ridicule. Laws touched on religious practices as well, and colonists could be punished for blasphemy, working on the Sabbath, or acting contemptuously toward a minister or interrupting him in his duties.

Despite strict laws that doled out punishment for even minor offenses and at times seemed designed to take the joy out of life, families in New Hampshire did find time for fun.

Colonial Recreation

With so much hard work to be done just to make a living, recreation was often combined with labor. For example, corn huskings and barn raisings were often followed by festive gatherings that included hearty meals, games, and sports such as wrestling. Visiting neighbors or relatives was a popular pastime, as were quilting bees for the women and shooting contests for the men.

Some things considered barbaric today were seen as entertainment in colonial times. Colonists gathered to view public whippings and even executions, while men wagered on dog and rooster fights.

Colonial children had few toys. Girls played with dolls, either homemade or, if a family was well off, imported from Europe. The prized possession for a colonial boy was his jackknife, which he could use to whittle whistles, wooden guns, and other playthings. Playing games was perhaps even more popular than playing with toys. Children enjoyed such active pursuits as barrel-hoop rolling, tag, top spinning, various ball games, and, in winter, ice skating on frozen streams and lakes. Boys challenged each other to games of marbles and girls played jacks, games that are still enjoyed today.

Punished for breaking the law, a colonist sits with his feet shackled in the stocks.

When the day's chores were done and time for play was over, for many New Hampshire children there was learning to be done.

Education in New Hampshire

When New Hampshire came under the administration of Massachusetts in 1641, it also fell under the jurisdiction of its laws. Education was an important part of life in Massachusetts, which founded the first American university, Harvard, in 1636. In 1647, the Massachusetts General Court passed an education law, which became known as the "Old Deluder Act" because it thwarted the devil, or "Old Deluder," who was believed to prey on the uneducated. This law required all towns of fifty or more families to have an elementary school. In addition, all towns of one hundred households or larger were required to have a grammar school (that is, a high school) to prepare students for university studies. The cost of education was borne mainly by the parents of the town. Sometimes a parcel of land was set aside as a "school-meadow" and the income from renting the land helped to pay the teacher's salary.

While most towns complied with education laws, some people diminished the value of an education. According to Jeremy Belknap "It was the interest of ignorant and unprincipled men to discourage literature because it would detract from their importance and expose them to contempt. The people in some places, being thus misled, thought it better to keep their children at work than provide schools for their instruction."[29]

Both boys and girls were taught reading, writing, and simple arithmetic. Early colonial children studied from a hornbook, which was a small piece of wood with a handle at the bottom. A piece of paper with the alphabet, simple syllables, and a prayer was attached to the wood and covered with a thin, clear piece of cow's horn. Students often wore these hornbooks by a string around their neck. The first real textbook was the eighty-page New England Primer, originally published in Boston in 1690. This little book, measuring only three inches by five inches, was used throughout the New England colonies for more than a century, with millions of copies

Children used hornbooks like this for their lessons in early colonial schoolhouses.

being printed. The New England Primer taught children to read using simple rhymes and woodcut pictures that generally had biblical themes. For example, the alphabet was taught in verse from A ("In Adam's Fall/We sinned all") to Z ("Zaccheus he/Did climb the Tree/Our Lord to see"). Religious teachings throughout the primer included a catechism that taught church doctrine in a series of questions and answers.

For most colonial children education did not go beyond the basics. For girls, especially, education was considered less important than learning such domestic skills as cooking and sewing. Abigail

Reverend Wheelock's College

Dartmouth College, one of today's leading institutions of higher learning, began because of one man's desire to bring knowledge and Christian values to Native American youth. Reverend Eleazar Wheelock was a Congregational minister who in 1753 established Moor's Indian Charity School in Connecticut. The school was founded with the idea that educated Native American children would be more receptive to the gospel. One of Wheelock's earliest and most successful students was a Native American named Samson Occom, who became an ordained minister and missionary to the Montauk and Mohegan tribes.

Intent on expanding his school into a seminary for training Native American missionaries, Wheelock sent Occom on a fund-raising journey to England in 1765. The trip raised some £12,000, a substantial amount that was managed by a board of trustees headed by William Legge, the Second Earl of Dartmouth. Needing more space for his growing school, Wheelock decided to move it to Hanover, New Hampshire, a small town on the banks of the Connecticut River. Governor John Wentworth granted a large parcel of land as the site for the school. On December 13, 1769, the new college, named for Lord Dartmouth, was officially chartered by the king of England. In 1771, Dartmouth's first graduating class, which consisted of four students, received its diplomas. Among those earning degrees was Eleazar Wheelock's son John, who would succeed his father as president of the college in 1779.

A controversy erupted in 1815 when New Hampshire, claiming Dartmouth's 1769 charter invalid, took control of the college. Ultimately the U.S. Supreme Court upheld the legality of the original charter, and Dartmouth remained a private institution. Today, more than five thousand students attend Dartmouth College, New Hampshire's most distinguished educational institution and the last American college to be established under colonial rule.

Adams, wife of President John Adams, wrote in 1817 that "My early education did not partake of the abundant opportunities which the present days offer, and which even our common country schools now afford. . . . Female education, in the best of families, went no further than writing and arithmetic; in some few and rare instances music and dancing."[30] But institutions of higher education did exist in New Hampshire. Dartmouth College was founded in 1769 in Hanover by Eleazar Wheelock, a Congregational minister who had established a school for Native American children in Connecticut. In 1781, Phillips Exeter Academy, a college preparatory school, was founded in the town of Exeter.

Life in colonial New Hampshire took a special breed of person, the kind Jeremy Belknap wrote so extensively about: "Firmness of nerve, patience in fatigue, intrepidity in danger and alertness in action, are to be numbered among their native and essential characteristics."[31] Indeed, these were the characteristics of a people who were willing to fight for their beliefs and for their independence.

Chapter Four

New Hampshire in the Revolution

The weather on December 13, 1774, was about as raw and miserable as a New England winter could get. Deep snow covered the ground and a sudden cold snap had frozen the primitive roads into rock-hard pathways of jagged ruts and hazardous furrows. Under a lowering sky a lone rider mounted his horse and set out from Boston, heading north along the road to Portsmouth, New Hampshire. He rode swiftly for he carried important news for the New Hampshire Whigs (patriots who advocated American independence): British troops were on their way to Portsmouth.

After delivering his message, the rider from Boston mounted his horse and headed for home. Four months later this same horseman would make his famous "midnight ride" to warn the citizens of Lexington and Concord, Massachusetts, that the British were coming. But Paul Revere's ride to Portsmouth that cold December foreshadowed the important role New Hampshire would play in the American Revolution.

The Road to Revolution

During the administrations of Benning Wentworth and his nephew John, New Hampshire grew in both prosperity and population.

On April 19, 1775, Paul Revere made his famous "midnight ride."

Although still one of the smaller colonies in terms of inhabitants, the number of towns had risen from the original four to almost 150 by 1773. Unlike the governors of other colonies, the two Wentworths were generally liked and respected by their citizens, and for more than thirty years they governed the thriving colony. But by the middle of the eighteenth century the winds of change were blowing through England's holdings in America, winds that hinted of turmoil, even revolution. It wouldn't take long for those winds to reach New Hampshire.

Fighting the French and Indian War had been costly for Great Britain, and they needed a way to replenish their exhausted coffers. At the same time, Britain wanted to exert more control over their subjects across the sea, who had lately grown restless under the authority of the mother country. In 1764, the Currency Act was passed, forbidding colonies to issue paper money. That same year the Sugar Act imposed a duty on numerous imported items, from sugar and molasses to animal hides and Persian silks. The Quartering Act of 1765 required colonists to make lodging available for British troops. The colonists bristled over these oppressive laws. In the spring of 1765, Parliament passed the Stamp Act, which required a tax stamp to be placed on newspapers, marriage licenses, and numerous other contracts and documents. Even such items as playing cards and school diplomas were required to have a stamp. Colonists, outraged by this new tax, circulated anti-stamp petitions and staged demonstrations throughout the colonies.

Tea and Redcoats

The stamp tax was not the last tax to be levied. Tea, the most popular drink in the colonies, had been heavily taxed since 1767. On December 16, 1773, Massachusetts patriots dressed as Native Americans dumped crates of British tea into Boston Harbor, an act of protest that came to be called the Boston Tea Party. The next year two shipments of tea arrived in Portsmouth, but there would be no repeat of what had occurred in Boston. Despite a small protest and a few broken windows in a tea merchant's house, the tea was allowed to be reshipped to Halifax in Canada. This relatively peaceful

In 1765, Parliament passed the Stamp Act, requiring colonists to use a tax stamp like these on all important documents.

Dressed like Native Americans, rebellious colonists dumped crates of British tea into the Boston Harbor.

reaction to the British tea was due in part to the good relations that Governor John Wentworth had maintained with the citizens of New Hampshire. But those relations were about to deteriorate, a situation caused in no small measure by the governor himself.

British troops had been garrisoned in Boston to counteract the revolutionary spirit brewing there. General Thomas Gage, commander of the British forces in America, was constantly adding more troops, and by late 1774 there were some four thousand redcoats, or British soldiers, in the city. Such a massive force created problems, as Jeremy Belknap relates: "The troops in Boston wanted barracks, to secure them against the approaching winter. The artificers [skilled craftsmen] of the town, were, by the popular voice, restrained from working in the

George Meserve—Colonial Tax Collector

After Britain passed the Stamp Act it needed agents in the colonies to sell the stamps. As Jeremy Belknap recounts in his *The History of New-Hampshire*, "The person appointed distributor of the stamps for New-Hampshire was George Meserve.... He received his appointment in England, and soon after embarked for America, and arrived at Boston." Before Meserve set foot on shore, however, he discovered that being a tax collector in the colonies would not be a popular occupation. "Before he landed," Belknap continues, "he was informed of the opposition which was making to the act; and that it would be acceptable to the people if he would resign, which he readily did, and they welcomed him on shore."

A different kind of welcome awaited him in Portsmouth. Citizens outraged with the stamp tax had made effigies, or dummies, of Meserve, the British prime minister, and the devil. They paraded these dummies through the streets of the town in protest. When Meserve finally arrived in Portsmouth he encountered the angry crowd and was forced to resign once more. By now Meserve was probably tired of resigning. But he would be made to renounce his post one more time when his official commission arrived.

By these actions New Hampshire and the rest of the colonies announced to Britain that the Stamp Act would not be tolerated when it went into effect on November 1, 1765. The protests worked, and in March 1766, the hated act was repealed. And what of poor George Meserve? He eventually fled the country and died an impoverished man in England, forever remembered as an "enemy of America."

service of government. General Gage was therefore obliged to send for assistance to the neighboring governors and, among others, to Governor Wentworth."[32]

John Wentworth realized all too well that supplying workers to build British barracks would antagonize his subjects. As an officer of the Crown, however, he knew he must do his duty. Wentworth hired the carpenters for Gage and tried to keep secret what their work in Boston would be. But the secret was not kept and when it finally came out, the citizens of New Hampshire realized which side their governor would take if revolution came. The beginning of that revolution sounded in New Hampshire a few months later from the pounding hooves of Paul Revere's horse.

Seizing Fort William and Mary

Paul Revere, Boston silversmith and patriot, galloped into Portsmouth on the afternoon of December 13, 1774. Upon his arrival a meeting of the town's Committee of Correspondence was called and Revere gave his report. The news was not good. Two British regiments, Revere told the committee, were sailing to Portsmouth to secure the stores of gunpowder at Fort William and Mary, a royal fortress located at New Castle in Portsmouth Harbor. In addition, further shipments of gunpowder and arms into the colonies would be prohibited. Without such ammunition a revolution would be snuffed out before it began.

As Paul Revere remounted his horse to return to Boston, neither he nor the Portsmouth committee could know that Revere's information was wrong. The British troops were actually heading for Massachusetts to supplement General Thomas Gage's forces there. Still, the committee wasted no time in organizing a response to Revere's news. The next morning, a crowd began to gather and around two hundred men and boys were soon marching along to the beat of a drum sounding the call through the streets of Portsmouth. By three o'clock an angry mob of some four hundred from Portsmouth and the surrounding towns had assembled to begin an assault on Fort William and Mary. Captain John Langdon led the charge.

Inside the fort, the English garrison, which consisted of exactly five men and their commanding officer, Captain John Cochran, prepared for battle. With a disadvantage of four hundred to six, the outcome was never in doubt. "I did all in my power to defend the fort," Captain Cochran wrote to Governor Wentworth, "but all my efforts could not avail against so great a number."[33] Several shots were fired before the New Hampshire men overpowered the garrison and tore down the British flag. They broke into the powder magazine and seized about one hundred barrels of gunpowder, which were then hidden in various locations around New Hampshire. The next day the men returned to the fort under the command of Major John Sullivan and made off with fifteen cannons and some small arms.

In April 1775, the battles of Lexington and Concord would become the opening skirmishes of the American Revolution. But for New Hampshire, the raid on Fort William and Mary four months earlier was the first battle in the war for independence. As the hostilities between the British and the colonists escalated, the New Hampshire militia prepared to enter the fighting.

Colonists carry barrels of gunpowder after seizing Fort William and Mary.

The Fighting Militia

When Governor John Wentworth learned of the raid on Fort William and Mary, he sent for the militia to oppose the attackers. Each colony had a loosely organized military force, or militia, made up of all the able-bodied men living in the colony. Under the control of the governor, a colony's militia could be called out in times of trouble to provide needed defense. Wentworth had built up New Hampshire's militia during his tenure as governor in order to protect New Hampshire against, as he put it, "invasion by His Majesty's enemies."[34] But public sentiment was turning against the governor, in part due to his sending the carpenters to Boston. Now, when he needed to muster his militia in response to the threat on Fort William and Mary, the men refused to obey his orders. Six months later, a mob would force Governor John Wentworth to flee his home in Portsmouth. He spent the rest of his life in Canada, never again setting foot in the colony he loved.

After the raid on Fort William and Mary, Major Sullivan began drilling the Portsmouth militia, a scene repeated throughout the colony in preparation for the hostilities which were now inevitable. Although they were a ragtag bunch with no uniforms and carried a variety of weapons, the men of the New Hampshire militia were ready to fight for independence. On April 19, 1775, that fight began when the first shots were fired at Lexington and Concord, two small Massachusetts towns. Historian George Morison describes how the citizen-soldiers of Peterborough, New Hampshire, took up arms:

> News of the Lexington battle fell upon them like a sudden trump from heaven summoning them to conflict. "We all set out," said one man, "with what weapons we could get, going like a flock of wild geese, we hardly knew why or whither." The word came to Capt. Thomas Morison at daylight, that the regulars were upon the road. In two hours, with his son and hired man, he was on his way to meet them, they on foot, he on horseback, with a large baking of bread, which had just been taken from the oven, in one end of the bag, and pork in the other.[35]

Answering the call to arms, New Hampshire men and boys, carrying the family musket, headed toward Boston.

From all over New Hampshire men and boys answered the call, wearing homespun clothes and carrying the family musket, a powder horn slung over one shoulder. They headed toward Boston, which was then occupied by some five thousand British soldiers. By June 1775, two New Hampshire regiments were in Massachusetts, training for an eventual fight with the British redcoats. On June 17, 1775, the famous Battle of Bunker Hill began.

All The King's Men

Charlestown peninsula, a strategic finger of land stretching between the Mystic and Charles Rivers just north of Boston, was unoccupied by either British or colonial troops. British general Thomas Gage planned to seize the peninsula; he knew that if colonial troops got there first, his hold on Boston would be jeopardized. But somehow Gage's plan leaked out to Americans in Boston. On the night of June 16, 1775, soldiers from Massachusetts and Connecticut

The *Ranger* and the Flag

By the beginning of the revolution, Portsmouth had been a colonial shipbuilding center for more than a century. Three warships were commissioned for the fledgling Continental Navy: the *Raleigh*, the *America*, and the *Ranger*. Originally called the *Hampshire*, the *Ranger* was renamed in honor of New Hampshire's elite force in the French and Indian War, Rogers' Rangers. The *Ranger* had three square-rigged masts and carried an armament of eighteen guns that could fire nine-pound cannonballs. About 110 feet long, she carried a crew of 150 men and officers under the command of John Paul Jones. Coincidentally on June 14, 1777, the same day that Jones received his commission to command the *Ranger*, the design for the first American flag was also approved.

While the *Ranger* was being finished, Jones set about to find sailors for his new command. He posted handbills with the bold words GREAT ENCOURAGEMENT FOR SEAMEN to attract potential crewmen, the first known use of a recruiting poster for the U. S. Navy. By November 1, 1777, Jones had his crew, and the *Ranger* set sail for France (to deliver important dispatches), the first naval vessel to fly the new American flag. Legend has it that the flag was made by women of Portsmouth using their petticoats for material. While this can't be confirmed, it does add a homespun touch to the story of the *Ranger* and the flag.

marched to the peninsula and under cover of darkness began digging a fortification on a rise called Breed's Hill. They had been ordered to occupy nearby Bunker Hill, but chose Breed's Hill instead because it was closer to Boston and thus within cannon shot of the British enemy.

The morning of June 17 dawned warm and bright, revealing to British eyes the work that the rebels had done. They had built redoubt, or reinforced earthen fortification, at the top of Breed's Hill, where they now waited for the fighting to begin. "We worked there undiscovered," wrote a colonial private, "till about five in the morn, and then we saw our danger, being against eight ships of the line and all Boston fortified against us."[36]

As they nervously waited for the fighting to begin, the colonial troops were encouraged by the sight of Colonel John Stark of the New Hampshire militia leading his regiments onto Charlestown peninsula. A tough, forty-six-year-old veteran of the French and Indian War, Stark had seen action with Rogers' Rangers, New Hampshire's legendary fighting force. From atop Bunker Hill, Stark quickly determined where his men were needed most: on the left flank of the redoubt, where troops from the Connecticut militia, positioned behind a rail fence, awaited the British assault. Stark's troops gathered hay to reinforce the meager protection provided by the fence, and hastily built a waist-high stone wall to cover a gap between the end of the fence and the river. Taking their position behind the fence the troops loaded their muskets with, some believe, gunpowder seized during the raid on Fort William and Mary. Then they hunkered down in anticipation of the redcoats' arrival. They would not have long to wait.

The first wave of British soldiers came marching to the beat of a drum, their weapons clanking rhythmically as they marched. When the enemy was within about fifty yards of his line, Stark gave the order to fire. A deafening volley of musket fire mowed down the first line of redcoats, and a second advance a moment later, and then a third. In all, ninety-six redcoats were killed in this first skirmish. At the redoubt on top of Breed's Hill other colonial troops, mostly from Massachusetts, were fighting back the British advance in a similar slaughter.

The first assault on Breed's Hill by the mighty British army had been repulsed by a group of colonial farmers and shopkeepers who were more experienced shooting at game than at enemy soldiers. Twice more the redcoats would advance on Breed's Hill. Only on the third assault, when the colonials were almost out of ammunition and forced into hand-to-hand combat with the redcoats did the colonials withdraw, leaving the Charlestown peninsula in British hands. The New Hampshire men conducted themselves courageously, continuing to fire as long as their ammunition held out. Even British general John Burgoyne remarked that Colonel Stark's "retreat was no flight; it was even covered with bravery and military skill."[37]

Though the British were victorious at the Battle of Bunker Hill, they lost over one thousand troops to the American revolutionaries.

The British had won what became known as the Battle of Bunker Hill. But it was, as a British general said, "A dear bought victory, another such would have ruined us."[38] Of about 2,300 British troops engaged in the battle, 1,054 were killed or wounded. The colonial militias had fielded some 1,500 to 1,700 troops and sustained casualties of 400 to 450. Although the statistics can be disputed, New Hampshire may have lost from 90 to 110 men out of a force of 700 to 1,000 troops. What is beyond dispute is the fact that the soldiers of New Hampshire played a pivotal role in the Battle of Bunker Hill.

Action at Bennington

Bunker Hill wasn't the last time that New Hampshire men would see combat in the American Revolution. And it wasn't the last the British would see of John Stark. In the summer of 1777, General Burgoyne needed supplies and horses to replenish his army as it marched south from Canada to New York. He knew just where to get them: the wilderness area west of New Hampshire, which would eventually become the state of Vermont. Fearing an invasion, Vermont asked neighboring states for help. In response, New Hampshire's John Stark, who had resigned from the Continental Army after being passed over for a promotion, quickly assembled a force of some fifteen hundred men. By early August, Stark's regiment, along with several hundred men of the Vermont militia, arrived at the town of Bennington to protect the supply depot there.

Opposing Stark was a detachment of eight hundred troops made up of British and Canadian soldiers, German mercenaries (called

John Stark led the colonists to a resounding victory over the British at the Battle of Bennington.

Hessians), and Native Americans, led by German colonel Friedrich Baum. When Baum's troops dug a defensive position on a hill a few miles west of Bennington, Stark decided to attack. On August 16, 1777, Stark's New Hampshire troops and the Vermont militia quickly surrounded and overran the enemy position, chasing the retreating soldiers and mortally wounding Baum.

The defeat at Bennington was a disaster for Burgoyne. Not only were nearly one thousand soldiers killed or captured, he failed to secure the supplies he desperately needed. John Stark's resounding victory at Bennington was the beginning of the end for Burgoyne, who surrendered two months later at Saratoga.

War at Sea

In December 1775, Britain passed the Prohibitory Act, which made all American ships subject to seizure by vessels of the Royal Navy. In retaliation, the Continental Congress began issuing "letters of marque" authorizing Americans to arm and outfit private ships to attack British merchant shipping. Portsmouth became a center for this activity, and by 1776 about one hundred "privateers" were sailing up and down the New England coast looking for vulnerable British vessels. Privateering could be a lucrative business, as a privateer's captain and crew shared the profits from captured ships and their cargoes. But it could also be dangerous, for privateers risked being captured and imprisoned or even hung as pirates by the British.

During the war, colonial privateers seized some six hundred British vessels. In a letter written in 1778, Dr. Josiah Bartlett, a signer of the Declaration of Independence, commented, "I think experience has shown that privateers have done more towards distressing the trade of our enemies and furnishing these states with necessaries, than Continental ships of the same force, and that it is in my opinion the greatest advantage we can at present expect from our navy."[39] Portsmouth shipbuilders did their part to outfit that navy by constructing several colonial warships including the *Raleigh*, one of the first vessels commissioned by the Continental Navy, and John Paul Jones's flagship, the *Ranger*.

The American victory at the Battle of Yorktown on October 19, 1781, signaled the end of the American Revolution. Of all the thirteen colonies, New Hampshire was the only one in which no battles were fought. But New Hampshire nevertheless played a vital role in the war for independence, providing arms and men from Bunker Hill to Yorktown. Some four thousand to five thousand New Hampshire men took part in Revolutionary War battles, and two generals, John Stark and John Sullivan, became important leaders during the war. But with the end of hostilities came the realization that a new nation had been born and was now waiting for its citizens to give it form and direction. While fighting a war had been difficult, forging a nation would prove to be equally demanding.

Chapter Five

A Nation United

The war was over. Hostilities had officially ended on October 19, 1781, with the surrender of the British commander, Lord Cornwallis, at Yorktown, Virginia. With the signing of the Treaty of Paris on September 3, 1783, the thirteen states, for they were indeed no longer colonies, celebrated their hard-won freedom from the British Crown. In Portsmouth, New Hampshire, as in other towns and villages throughout America, cannons boomed and church bells rang out the jubilant news of independence. People flocked to the North Church for thanksgiving services, spent a festive afternoon filled with speeches, toasts, and banquets, then ended the day watching fireworks burst in the sky over their newly independent land.

The American Revolution had successfully freed the colonies from British rule and established a new government on American soil. But much work needed to be done to forge the new states into a true nation. "It remained," wrote Jeremy Belknap, "to accommodate the minds and manners of the people, under the new administration, to a regular course of justice, both public and private; to perfect the union of the States; and to establish a system of finance. These things were necessary to make the revolution complete."[40] The chain of events required to complete the revolution had begun even before the war ended.

A Weak Confederation

The battles of Lexington, Concord, and Bunker Hill were over and the colonies had declared their independence. After July 4, 1776, they sought a way to join together as a nation and pursue their quest for freedom. A committee of the Second Continental Congress drew up the Articles of Confederation, by which the states "hereby severally enter into a firm league of friendship with each other, for their common defense, the security of their liberties, and their mutual and general welfare."[41] After much debate and many revisions, the Articles were presented to the states for ratification on November 15, 1777. It took more than three years for all the states to approve the Articles, which finally took effect on March 1, 1781.

As its name indicates, the Articles of Confederation bound the states together in a "confederation" or alliance that allowed each state to retain its own sovereignty. But this alliance was a weak one.

General George Washington's deputy (on white horse) receives the British surrender after the Redcoats' defeat at Yorktown.

While it could create an army and navy, which were necessary to fight the war, it had neither an executive branch nor courts to create laws and administer justice. The confederation could not regulate foreign trade or collect taxes, but relied instead on the good faith of the states to pay the expenses of running the country. After the war many states simply ignored Congress's "requisitions," or pleas for payment. Among these recalcitrant states was New Hampshire which, according to one incensed writer from Virginia "has not paid a shilling since peace and does not ever mean to pay one to all eternity."[42]

A committee of the Second Continental Congress drew up the Articles of Confederation, declaring the states' alliance.

In the years following the Revolution it had become increasingly clear that the Articles of Confederation were not strong enough to make the United States truly united. A new means of governing the nation had to be found, and in May 1787, men began gathering in Philadelphia to try to figure out just what that means would be.

The Road to a Constitution

John Langdon and Nicholas Gilman were chosen to represent New Hampshire at the Federal Convention in Philadelphia. Langdon had been one of the leaders of the raid on Fort William and Mary, and was later elected state president (New Hampshire's original name for its governor) and the first U.S. senator from New Hampshire. Gilman had been an officer with the Third New Hampshire Regiment during the Revolution and, like Langdon, was active in politics, serving four terms in the House of Representatives. Since the state had no money to underwrite their trip, Langdon paid their expenses out of his own pocket. When the two men entered Philadelphia's State House, fifty-three delegates from twelve states (Rhode Island did not send representatives to the convention) were already hard at work. Although a good deal of progress on a federal constitution had already been made, much remained to be done.

As the long, hot summer wore on, discussions at the convention ranged from representation in Congress (that is, whether smaller states should have as much influence as the larger ones), to the differences between northern and southern states on the subject of slavery, to just how much power the federal government should have over the individual states. Both John Langdon and Nicholas Gilman believed that the United States should have a strong federal government. Langdon, a wealthy merchant, endorsed the constitution because of its authority to regulate interstate and international commerce, and its ability to provide economic stability for the nation. Gilman, too, advocated what he called a "high-toned monarchy,"[43] meaning a powerful centralized government with a strong president (not a king as the term "monarchy" might imply). However, while he dutifully attended every session and voted when required, Gilman remained quiet during the floor debates.

By September 17, the debates were over and the delegates gathered in the east room of the State House to sign the new Constitution. After all had affixed their signatures, the Federal Convention was adjourned. The next day Nicholas Gilman reflected on the importance of their work in a letter to his cousin: "It was done by bargain and compromise, yet notwithstanding its imperfections, on the adoption of it depends (in my feeble judgment) whether or no we shall become a respectable nation, or a people torn to pieces by intestine [internal] commotions, and rendered contemptible for ages."[44]

The Keystone

On February 13, 1788, delegates from all over New Hampshire gathered at the courthouse in Exeter to discuss ratification of the Constitution. Even though by this time six other states had voted to accept the Constitution, the New Hampshire convention was determined to put the matter to a full debate. John Langdon and Nicholas Gilman were Federalists, delegates who supported ratification of the new Constitution. Federalists felt that joining the

Washington's Visit to New Hampshire

As the first president of a new political entity called the United States of America, George Washington must have wondered just how united the states really were. Could these thirteen former colonies really act together as a unified country? As president it was Washington's duty to find out, and so he planned to tour each of the states, to meet the people, and to use his popularity to consolidate the new confederation into a cohesive nation.

For four weeks in the fall of 1789 Washington toured New England, arriving in New Hampshire on October 31. The following account of his reception upon reaching Portsmouth is taken from Washington's private diary and can be found on the SeacoastNH website (www.seacoastnh.com/brewster/52.html):

Here I ... was received by the President of the State of New Hampshire [John Sullivan], the Vice President, some of the Council, Messrs. Langdon and Wingate of the Senate, Col. Parker, Marshal of the State, and many other respectable characters; beside several troops of well-clothed horse [mounted soldiers], in handsome uniforms, and many officers of the militia, also in handsome (white and red) uniforms, of the manufacture of the State. With this cavalcade we proceeded, and arrived before three o'clock at Portsmouth, where we were received with every token of respect and appearance of cordiality under a discharge of artillery. The streets, doors and windows were crowded here, as at all other places; and, alighting at the Town House, odes were sung and played in honor of the President. The same happened yesterday at my entrance to Newburyport, being stopped at my entrance to hear it.

states in a federal union would have economic benefits and give the nation increased status with European governments.

Many of their fellow New Hampshire citizens, however, were opposed to adopting the Constitution. These "Antifederalists" were afraid that under a federal constitution, the interests of small states like New Hampshire would be neglected by a distant national government. They also objected to the Constitution's conditions on length of congressional terms and a religious test as a prerequisite for holding office. Feelings ran high between the two opposing camps. John Sullivan, also a Federalist delegate, described the Antifederalists in a letter to Nicholas Gilman as "a motley mixture of ancient Torys . . . persons in debt, distress, and poverty, either real or imaginary; men of blind piety, hypocrites and bankrupts; together with many honest men bound by instructions to vote against the constitution at all events."[45]

During the deliberations it became increasingly clear that the Federalists did not have enough votes to approve the constitution. So they made a deal with undecided delegates to adjourn the session before a vote could be taken. Another meeting was then scheduled to convene in June. In the meantime, the Federalists would try to convince the undecided delegates to support the Constitution. On June 18, 1788, the delegates assembled once more, this time at the Old North Church in Concord. Spectators filled the galleries to witness the historic proceedings. After several days of deliberation, the Federalists were still unsure if they had the majority necessary for ratification. But on Saturday, June 21 the time came to put the Constitution to a vote. "Whilst the Secretary was calling over the members," wrote Portsmouth historian Nathaniel Adams, "and recording their votes, a death-like silence prevailed; every bosom throbbed with anxious expectation."[46] Finally, at one o'clock the votes were tallied: fifty-seven delegates had voted for the Constitution, forty-seven against. The Federalists breathed a sigh of relief; the Constitution had been approved. Even the most outspoken Antifederalist, delegate Joshua Atherton from Amherst, eventually conceded that "it is adopted, let us try it."[47]

After several months of discussion and debate, the constitution was approved and signed by the delegates of the newly formed United States.

New Hampshire's approval of the Constitution assured the state a unique place in American history. The Constitution required the approval of nine states before becoming official. As the ninth state to ratify (beating out Virginia by only four days), New Hampshire, John Langdon wrote to George Washington, was "placing the Key Stone in the great arch"[48] of the federal government. When the news of ratification reached Portsmouth a parade was organized, which included marchers proudly representing their trades: from farmers, millers, and masons to clockmakers, silversmiths, and physicians. Here were the people of New Hampshire from laborers to town officials. And ahead of them lay the job of making their state a vital part of the newly formed union.

A New Century Dawns

With the new Constitution finally in place, a turbulent quarter-century of war and political uncertainty had come to an end. A new era of hope was beginning. New Hampshire historian Jeremy Belknap described his satisfaction and relief that the years of revolutionary turmoil were over. "I hope that twenty-five years of controversy and revolution will be sufficient for the space of time I have to exist on the globe. Were I to live to the age of Methusaleh, I should not wish to see another such period."[49] But although one period of turmoil had ended, it left another in its wake.

The cost of the war caused mounting debt in New Hampshire as well as in the other states, triggering a depression during the

Josiah Bartlett

Josiah Bartlett was born in Amesbury, Massachusetts in 1729. He began studying medicine at age sixteen and after five years of apprenticing with a physician relative, he moved to Kingston, New Hampshire. There his medical practice grew, as did his reputation for not being bound to traditional methods of healing. When he fell ill with a life-threatening fever in 1752 he treated himself with cold cider rather than the standard remedy of the time, hot liquids. To the astonishment of his peers, he fully recovered. Practicing medicine, however, was only a part of Bartlett's busy life.

In 1765, he was commissioned a justice of the peace by Governor Benning Wentworth, a position through which the governor sought to influence Bartlett. He would later lose this post because of his support of the patriot cause. He was also a lieutenant commander in the New Hampshire militia and served in the legislature from 1765 to the eve of the Revolution. As the senior New Hampshire delegate to the Continental Congress in 1776, Josiah Bartlett was honored to cast the first vote for independence, since the delegates voted in order beginning with the northernmost states. In 1790, Bartlett became the chief executive of New Hampshire, an office that was at first called president and later changed to governor. He served for four years until his retirement due to failing health and died on May 19, 1795.

postwar years. The value of paper money issued by the Continental Congress fluctuated wildly, and restrictions on American trade to British ports brought on further hardships. This economic depression added to the difficulties of poor people trying to make a living in New Hampshire. In September 1786, about two hundred beleaguered farmers marched to the capital at Exeter where the state legislature was meeting and demanded that something be done to relieve their financial problems. The crowd remained until dusk, when the threat of armed intervention by the militia caused them to quickly disperse.

In Portsmouth, foreign trade, the lifeblood of the town, had been interrupted by the war, causing hardships on rich and poor alike. But these hardships seemed to bring the people closer together with the realization that only with the cooperation of all its citizens could Portsmouth regain its former prosperity. During the 1790s, prosperity would indeed return to the town with the building of new houses, the repairing of aging schools and churches, and an increase in trade.

According to the census of 1800, New Hampshire's population was 183,858 at the beginning of the nineteenth century. While this was a substantial increase since 1780 when the state had some 88,000 people, New Hampshire was still small compared to such states as Massachusetts, Pennsylvania, and Connecticut. During the previous century most New Hampshireites had lived in the coastal area, where they engaged in commerce such as fishing, shipbuilding, and other trades. Portsmouth, at the mouth of the Piscataqua River, was the state's largest town with about 5,400 residents at the turn of the century.

Yet the vast expanse of central and western New Hampshire, abundant in unoccupied land and natural resources, drew more and more people to move west. As the fertile earth of the Merrimack and Connecticut River valleys was gradually turned into cultivated farmland, farmers began moving toward the hills where rocky ground and thin soil made agriculture a challenge. Many farms failed, but hardy New Hampshireites continued their struggle to carve out a life in the west. In 1808, Concord, in the

Merrimack Valley, was made the state capital, an acknowledgment that New Hampshire's population was indeed moving west.

Agriculture, fishing, and lumbering were still the major industries of postrevolutionary New Hampshire, with about 80 percent of the people making their living from the land. But industry was beginning to make gradual inroads into the New

New Hampshireites work in one of the twelve textile mills operating in the state in the early nineteenth century.

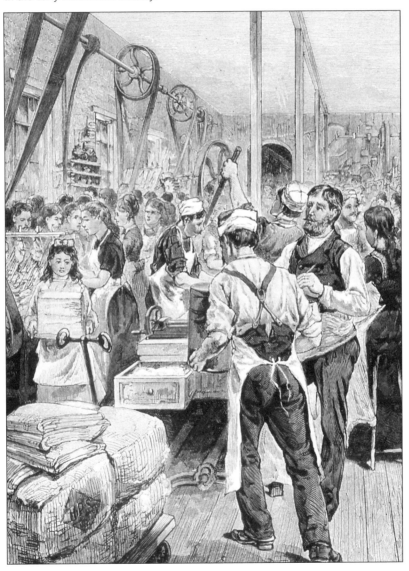

Hampshire economy. In 1803, the state's first cotton mill began operation on the Souhegan River at New Ipswich. A mill on the Amoskeag Falls in a town called Derryfield was built in 1805 and lured investors from New York and Boston. The mill also attracted many immigrant workers and as a result, Derryfield, renamed Manchester in 1846, eventually became the largest city in New Hampshire. By the end of the first decade of the nineteenth century, twelve textile mills powered by New Hampshire's abundant rivers and streams were operating in the state.

Governing the New State

As part of the new nation, each state came under the jurisdiction of the Constitution of the United States of America. But each state also needed a way to govern its internal workings. New Hampshire had adopted its first state constitution on January 5, 1776, seven months before the nation declared its independence from Britain. In doing so, it became the first of the thirteen states to become independent, with a separate official government. Meshech Weare, aging chairman of New Hampshire's Committee of Safety and often called "The Father of New Hampshire," acted as the executive head of the government. This temporary constitution remained in force for almost nine years until a permanent constitution was finally ratified in October 1783 and went into effect in June 1784. By an overwhelming vote, Meshech Weare became the state's first "president," as the head of New Hampshire's government was then known. When Weare's one-year term ended, John Langdon took over the office.

Many prominent men became New Hampshire's president, an office that was renamed governor in 1793. Langdon served six terms, as president and then governor of the state. John Sullivan, who stormed Fort William and Mary and had been a general under George Washington, served three terms as New Hampshire's president. John Taylor Gilman, the eldest son of Nicholas Gilman, held the office for a total of fourteen years, from 1794 to 1805 and 1813 to 1816.

John Langdon, New Hampshire's second president, administered the oath of office to George Washington.

Although a few prominent names—Captain John Mason, Nicholas Gilman, General John Stark, to mention just a few—reappear throughout the history of colonial New Hampshire, it was the common people, whose names will never be known, that gave the state its character.

People of the Granite State

High up in the Franconia Range of New Hampshire's ruggedly beautiful White Mountains, a craggy face looks out over a placid body of water called Profile Lake. Its features are sharply angular, this image of a man seen in profile, and it goes by many names: the Great Stone Face, the Profile, and most frequently, the Old Man of the Mountain.

He has been on this mountain for thousands of years, since the glaciers retreated and left behind this startlingly lifelike granite illusion. An illusion he surely is, for to look upon the mountain from another vantage point reveals only the rocky crags one would expect to see in the granite peaks of northern New Hampshire.

An illusion, yes, but also a symbol. For the Old Man of the Mountain's stern visage has come to symbolize the uncompromising qualities and hardworking endurance of the people of New Hampshire. Famed

For thousands of years, the Old Man of the Mountain has stood high in the Franconia Range and has come to symbolize New Hampshire.

statesman and orator Daniel Webster, a native of the state, once wrote that "Men hang out their signs indicative of their respective trades . . . but up in the mountains of New Hampshire, God Almighty has hung out a sign to show that there He makes men."[50] Those men—and women—are the settlers who braved an ocean voyage and primitive conditions on a new continent; the patriots who fought and bled for the country's freedom; and the ordinary citizens who lived, worked, and died achieving neither fame nor fortune. The strong, proud, and independent men and women of New Hampshire left behind a legacy upon which future generations would build a prosperous state and a mighty nation.

Notes

Introduction: "Live Free or Die"
1. Quoted in State of New Hampshire website: www.state.nh.us.nhinfo/emblem.html.
2. Quoted in State of New Hampshire web site: www.state.nh.us/nhinfo/emblem.html.

Chapter One: Early New Hampshire
3. Quoted in Steven F. Johnson, *Ninnuock (The People)*. Marlborough, MA: Bliss, 1995, p. 22.
4. Quoted in Time-Life Books, *Algonquians of the East Coast*. Alexandria, VA: Time-Life Books, 1995, p. 34.
5. Quoted in Johnson, *Ninnuock (The People)*, p. 91.
6. George Parker Winship, *Sailors' Narratives of Voyages Along the New England Coast, 1524–1624*. Boston: Houghton, Mifflin, 1905, pp. 54, 55.
7. Quoted in Parker River Clean Water Association website: www.parkerriver.org/pr_history/na_amer/champlai.htm.
8. Quoted in Parker River Clean Water Association web site: www.parkerriver.org/pr_history/na_amer/champlai.htm.
9. Jeremy Belknap, *The History of New-Hampshire*. 3 vols, 1792. Reprint, New York: Arno Press, 1972, vol. 1, p. 2.
10. John Smith, *A Description of New-England*. 1616. Reproduction, Washington, DC: P. Force, 1837, p. 1.
11. Quoted in J. A. Leo Lemay, *The American Dream of Captain John Smith*. Charlottesville: University Press of Virginia, 1991, p. 206.
12. Quoted in Michael Kraus, *The United States to 1865*. Ann Arbor: University of Michigan Press, 1959, p. 46.
13. Quoted in Richard Arthur Preston, *Gorges of Plymouth Fort*. Toronto: University of Toronto Press, 1953, p. 138.

Chapter Two: Founding the Colony

14. Smith, *A Description of New-England,* p. 21.
15. Quoted in Preston, *Gorges of Plymouth Fort,* p. 170.
16. Belknap, *The History of New-Hampshire,* vol. 1, p. 5.
17. Belknap, *The History of New-Hampshire,* vol. 1, pp. 5–6.
18. Quoted in Belknap, *The History of New-Hampshire,* vol. 1, p. 8.
19. Quoted in the Avalon Project website: www.yale.edu/lawweb/avalon/states/nh01.htm.
20. Belknap, *The History of New-Hampshire,* vol. 1, p. 18.
21. Quoted in Jere R. Daniell, *Colonial New Hampshire: A History.* Millwood, NY: KTO Press, 1981, pp. 24, 25.
22. Belknap, *The History of New-Hampshire,* vol. 1, pp. 38–39.
23. Belknap, *The History of New-Hampshire,* vol. 1, p. 169.

Chapter Three: Life in Colonial New Hampshire

24. Quoted in Belknap, *The History of New-Hampshire,* vol. 1, p. 19.
25. Belknap, *The History of New-Hampshire,* vol. 3, p. 209.
26. Belknap, *The History of New-Hampshire,* vol. 3, p. 210.
27. Quoted in Federal Writers' Project, *New Hampshire: A Guide to the Granite State.* 1938. Republished, St. Clair Shores, MI: Somerset, 1974, p. 37.
28. Quoted in Federal Writers' Project, *New Hampshire: A Guide to the Granite State,* p. 37.
29. Belknap, *The History of New-Hampshire,* vol. 3, p. 289.
30. Quoted in Alice Morse Earle, *Child Life in Colonial Days.* 1899. Reprint, Stockbridge, MA: Berkshire House, 1993, pp. 93–94.
31. Belknap, *The History of New-Hampshire,* vol. 3, p. 257.

Chapter Four: New Hampshire in the Revolution

32. Belknap, *The History of New-Hampshire,* vol. 2, p. 374.
33. Quoted in Anne Eastman and Charles Eastman Jr., "Raid on Fort William and Mary." *NH: Years of Revolution.* Profiles Publications and the NH Bicentennial Commission, 1976. Seacoast NH web site: www.seacoastnh.com/history/rev/willmary.html.
34. Quoted in Federal Writers' Project, *New Hampshire: A Guide*

to the Granite State, p. 40.

35. Quoted in Elizabeth Forbes Morison and Elting E. Morison, *New Hampshire: A Bicentennial History.* New York: W. W. Norton, 1976, p. 72.

36. Quoted in George F. Scheer and Hugh F. Rankin, *Rebels and Redcoats.* New York: World Publishing, 1957, p. 60.

37. Quoted in W. J. Wood, *Battles of the Revolutionary War, 1775–1781.* Chapel Hill, NC: Algonquin Books of Chapel Hill, 1990, p. 31.

38. Quoted in Scheer and Rankin, *Rebels and Redcoats,* p. 67.

39. Quoted in Frank C. Mevers, ed., *The Papers of Josiah Bartlett.* Hanover, NH: University Press of New England, 1979, p. 187.

Chapter Five: A Nation United

40. Belknap, *The History of New-Hampshire,* vol. 2, p. 459.

41. Quoted in Michael Kammen, ed., *The Origins of the American Constitution: A Documentary History.* New York: Penguin Books, 1986, p. 10.

42. Quoted in Catherine Drinker Bowen, *Miracle at Philadelphia.* Boston: Little, Brown, 1966, p. 5.

43. Quoted in Bowen, *Miracle at Philadelphia,* p. 188.

44. Quoted in Bowen, *Miracle at Philadelphia,* p. 254.

45. Quoted in William M. Gardner, Frank C. Mevers, and Richard F. Upton, eds., *New Hampshire: The State That Made Us a Nation.* Portsmouth, NH: Peter E. Randall, 1989, p. 33.

46. Quoted in Morison, *New Hampshire: A Bicentennial History,* p. 86.

47. Quoted in William M. Gardner, et al, eds., *New Hampshire: The State That Made Us a Nation,* p. 17.

48. Quoted in William M. Gardner, et al, eds., *New Hampshire: The State That Made Us a Nation,* p. 213.

49. Quoted in William M. Gardner, et al, eds., *New Hampshire: The State That Made Us a Nation,* p. 81.

50. Quoted in Vance Muse, *The Smithsonian Guide to Historic America: Northern New England.* New York: Stewart, Tabori, and Chang, 1998, p. 148.

Chronology

1603

Captain Martin Pring explores the mouth of the Piscataqua River.

1614

Captain John Smith sails along the New England coast.

1622

John Mason and Ferdinando Gorges receive grant of land in New England.

1623

Pannaway Plantation becomes the first permanent settlement in New Hampshire.

1629

John Mason receives a grant of land which he names New Hampshire.

1630

Strawbery Banke (Portsmouth) established.

1641

The three remaining towns that make up New Hampshire (Portsmouth, Exeter, and Dover) petition Crown to place themselves under Massachusetts rule.

1679

New Hampshire becomes a separate royal colony.

1756

Robert Rogers forms Rogers' Rangers to fight in the French and Indian War.

1769

Dartmouth College founded at Hanover.

1774

John Sullivan and John Langdon lead group of four hundred men to seize Fort William and Mary.

1775
New Hampshire men fight at Battle of Bunker Hill.

1776
Josiah Bartlett casts the first vote for independence.

1777
General John Stark leads New Hampshire troops to victory at the Battle of Bennington.

1783
New Hampshire state constitution is ratified.

1788
As the ninth state to vote for ratification, New Hampshire makes the U.S. Constitution official.

For Further Reading

Tracy Barnett, *Growing Up in Colonial America*. Brookfield, CT: Millbrook Press, 1995. The author takes readers back three hundred years to examine the lives of children in colonial America. Numerous period illustrations provide a visual reference to many aspects of life in the colonies.

Colin G. Calloway, *The Abenaki*. New York: Chelsea House, 1989. A complete history of the Abenaki of northern New England, this book examines their lives and relations with European settlers from earliest contact to the twentieth century.

Christopher Collier and James Lincoln Collier, *Creating the Constitution: 1787*. New York: Benchmark Books, 1999. Examines how the U.S. Constitution was created, from the Articles of Confederation to the Constitutional Convention in 1787, and the human rights underpinning this remarkable document.

Ruth Dean and Melissa Thomson, *Life in the American Colonies*. San Diego, CA: Lucent Books, 1999. This lively account tells how people from many different European cultures made a new life in a new world. Provides interesting details on colonial commerce, dress, government, and everyday life.

Edward Dolan, *The American Revolution: How We Fought the War of Independence*. Brookfield, CT: Millbrook Press, 1995. The author follows the course of the American Revolution from the opening shots at Lexington and Concord to the British surrender at Yorktown. Includes illustrations and maps.

Dennis B. Fradin, *The New Hampshire Colony*. Chicago: Childrens Press, 1988. This easy-to-read history of the New Hampshire colony includes numerous illustrations, profiles of important figures in New Hampshire history, and a colonial timeline.

Carter Smith, ed., *The Explorers and Settlers: A Sourcebook on Colonial America*. Brookfield, CT: Millbrook Press, 1991. This account of the adventurers who explored early America and settled in this uncharted land is illustrated with drawings, engravings, and maps.

R. Conrad Stein, *New Hampshire*. New York: Childrens Press, 2000. This book provides a good general overview of the state of New Hampshire and is filled with color photographs, maps, and fascinating state facts. It briefly covers the state's history before turning to modern-day New Hampshire.

C. Keith Wilbur, *The New England Indians*. Philadelphia: Chelsea House, 1997. An illustrated guide to the New England Indians spanning ten thousand years of history, this book includes detailed drawings of tools, weapons, dwellings, and other aspects of the New England Indian culture.

James Playsted Wood, *Colonial New Hampshire*. Nashville, KY: Thomas Nelson, 1973. This book presents a thorough and straightforward history of colonial New Hampshire and the events leading up to the Revolution. Includes a chronology and listing of historic sites in New Hampshire.

Karen Zeinert, ed., *Memoirs of Andrew Sherburne*. Hamden, CT: Linnet Books, 1993. Sherburne, a Portsmouth boy who joined the Continental Navy at age thirteen, recounts his life at sea including capture, shipwreck, illness, and the excitement of sea battles.

Works Consulted

Jeremy Belknap, *The History of New-Hampshire.* 3 vols, 1792. Reprint, New York: Arno Press, 1972. New Hampshire's first historian details the colony's growth including early exploration, settlement, and New Hampshire's struggle for independence.

Catherine Drinker Bowen, *Miracle at Philadelphia.* Boston: Little, Brown, 1966. A lively and detailed narrative of the Constitutional Convention in 1787. The book presents a day-by-day account of the proceedings and gives insight into the personalities of the men who framed the Constitution.

Jere R. Daniell, *Colonial New Hampshire: A History.* Millwood, NY: KTO Press, 1981. The author, a history professor at Dartmouth, presents a comprehensive account of New Hampshire's history from first exploration to the eve of the Revolution.

Alice Morse Earle, *Child Life in Colonial Days.* 1899. Reprint, Stockbridge, MA: Berkshire House, 1993. The author uses primary sources to provide a detailed description of childhood in colonial America. Covers everything from dress and education to work and play.

William M. Gardner, Frank C. Mevers, and Richard F. Upton, eds., *New Hampshire: The State That Made Us a Nation.* Portsmouth, NH: Peter E. Randall, 1989. This book was published for New Hampshire's bicentennial celebration of the signing of the U.S. Constitution.

Steven F. Johnson, *Ninnuock (The People).* Marlborough, MA: Bliss, 1995. An examination of all the New England Algonquian tribes from prehistory to the Revolution. The book includes a glossary of tribal names.

Michael Kammen, ed., *The Origins of the American Constitution: A Documentary History*. New York: Penguin Books, 1986. The author discusses the importance of several fundamental American documents including correspondence of the founding fathers, the Articles of Confederation, and the Constitution.

Michael Kraus, *The United States to 1865*. Ann Arbor: University of Michigan Press, 1959. A detailed recounting of American history from discovery to the end of the Civil War. Part of the University of Michigan's fifteen-volume *History of the Modern World*.

J. A. Leo Lemay, *The American Dream of Captain John Smith*. Charlottesville: University Press of Virginia, 1991. The story of John Smith as both a learned man and an intrepid explorer, with discussions of Smith's life in Europe, his expeditions, and his vision for a colonized America.

Frank C. Mevers, ed., *The Papers of Josiah Bartlett*. Hanover, NH: University Press of New England, 1979. A compilation of Bartlett's correspondence and other papers written between 1751 and 1784. Includes explanatory notes and a brief biographical introduction.

Elizabeth Forbes Morison and Elting E. Morison, *New Hampshire: A Bicentennial History*. New York: W. W. Norton, 1976. Written for the American Revolution Bicentennial, this book traces the history of New Hampshire from its colonial beginnings to its role as a modern-day state. Includes a photo-essay.

Vance Muse, *The Smithsonian Guide to Historic America: Northern New England*. New York: Stewart, Tabori and Chang, 1998. An illustrated travel guide to the northern New England states: Vermont, New Hampshire, and Maine. Includes interesting places to visit, short historical anecdotes, maps, and color photographs.

Richard Arthur Preston, *Gorges of Plymouth Fort*. Toronto: University of Toronto Press, 1953. Details of the life of Ferdinando Gorges, including his important role in the early colonization of New Hampshire.

George F. Scheer and Hugh F. Rankin, *Rebels and Redcoats*. New York: World Publishing, 1957. The battles of the Revolutionary War come alive through eyewitness accounts taken from diaries, letters, and battlefield reports.

John Smith, *A Description of New-England*. 1616. Reproduction, Washington, DC: P. Force, 1837. Captain Smith's own account of his explorations of New England. Provides fascinating first-person details of the exploration of New Hampshire and Smith's advocacy of colonization.

Time-Life Books, *Algonquians of the East Coast*. Alexandria, VA: Time-Life Books, 1995. This illustrated book, part of Time-Life's series, *The American Indians*, chronicles the culture, beliefs, and lifestyles of the Algonquian tribes.

George Parker Winship, compiler, *Sailors' Narratives of Voyages Along the New England Coast, 1524–1624*. Boston: Houghton, Mifflin, 1905. A compilation of accounts of exploration written by the explorers themselves. Includes accounts by Martin Pring, John Smith, Giovanni da Verrazano, and other early adventurers.

W. J. Wood, *Battles of the Revolutionary War, 1775–1781*. Chapel Hill, NC: Algonquin Books of Chapel Hill, 1990. A detailed recounting of the major battles of the Revolution. The author demonstrates that the Continental Army actually defeated the British, rather than merely outlasting them.

Works Progress Administration, Federal Writers' Project for the State of New Hampshire, *New Hampshire: A Guide to the Granite State*. 1938. Republished, St. Clair Shores, MI: Somerset, 1974. A classic work published as part of the Works Progress Administration writers' project. Although dated, it provides some interesting details of New Hampshire's growth in colonial times.

Internet Sources

Avalon Project, "Grant of Hampshire to Capt. John Mason, 7th of Novemr., 1629." www.yale.edu/lawweb/avalon/states/nh01.htm.

Anne Eastman and Charles Eastman Jr., "Raid on Fort William and Mary." *NH: Years of Revolution.* Profiles Publications and the NH Bicentennial Commission, 1976. Seacoast NH, www.seacoastnh.com/history/rev/willmary.html.

Parker River Clean Water Association, "Samuel de Champlain Explores Massachusetts' North Shore." www.parker-river.org/pr_history/na_amer/champlai.htm.

State of New Hampshire, "New Hampshire Almanac: State Emblem and Motto." www.state.nh.us/nhinfo/emblem.html.

Index

Bunker Hill, Battle of, 59–63
Burgoyne, 64

Cabot, John, 15
Caboto, Giovanni. *See* Cabot, John
Cartier, Jacques, 22
Champlain, Samuel de, 16–17
Charles I, 30
Charles II, 35, 44
Charlestown peninsula, 59–61
charms, 15
charters, 24
Church of England, 30
churches. *See* meetinghouses
Cochran, John, 57
Committee of Safety, 76
Concord, 71, 74–75
  Battle of, 57–58
Congregational Church, 43
Connecticut, 59
Connecticut River, 49, 74
Constitution, 10, 68–73, 76
Continental Army, 63
Continental Congress, 64, 74
Continental Navy, 60, 64
Cornwallis, Lord, 66
Council for New England, 24–25, 27
Currency Act (1764), 52
Cutt, John, 35

Dartmouth College, 40, 49–50
Dawnland, people of the. *See* Wabanaki
Declaration of Independence, 9
Derryfield. *See* Manchester
Description of New England, A (Smith), 23
Discoverer (ship), 16
dog fights, 45
dolls, 46
Dover, 25, 31–32, 44

Episcopalians, 43
executions, 45
Exeter, 30–32, 50, 70

Father of New Hampshire. *See* Weare, Meshech
Federal Convention, 68–69
Federalists, 71
Federal Writers' Project, 20
forests, 37–40
Fort William and Mary, 56–58
Frances (ship), 17
Franconia Range, 77
French and Indian War, 33, 52

Gage, Thomas, 54–56, 59
General Court, 32–35
Gilman, John Taylor, 76
Gilman, Nicholas, 68–69, 71, 76–77
Gorges, Ferdinando, 21–22, 24, 27–29
governors, 44–45
Great Stone Face. *See* Old Man of the Mountain

Hampshire. See Ranger
Hampton, 31
Hanover, 49
Harvard University, 40, 47
Henry VII, 15
Hessians, 64
Hilton, Edward and William, 25
Hilton's Point, 25
History of New-Hampshire (Belknap), 25, 37
hornbooks, 47
House of Representatives, 69

ice skating, 46
Isles of Shoals, 16, 18, 23

jackknives, 46
jacks, 46

Index

Picture Credits

Cover Photo: © Ralph Crosby Smith/Wood River Gallery/Picture Quest

© Bettmann/CORBIS, 31, 44, 52, 59, 72, 77

Hulton/Archive by Getty Images, 17, 26, 32, 54, 62, 67, 68

Chris Jouan, 9

Library of Congress, 23

New Hampshire Office of Emergency Management, 78

© North Wind Pictures, 12, 16, 19, 28, 34, 38, 39, 41, 42, 53, 57, 75

© Stock Montage, 14, 46, 48, 63

About the Author

Craig E. Blohm has been writing magazine articles on historical subjects for children for more than fifteen years. He has also written for social studies textbooks and has conducted workshops in writing history for children. A native of Chicago, he has worked for more than twenty-five years in the field of television production as writer, producer, and director. He is currently the television and radio production coordinator at Purdue University Calumet in Hammond, Indiana. He and his wife, Desiree, live in Tinley Park, Illinois and have two sons, Eric and Jason.